DORON ALMOG

The Commitment

A Study of the Impact of American Jews on the
Establishment of the State of Israel
1945-1949

Contento de Semrik

The Commitment

Doron Almog

Senior Editors & Producers: Contento de Semrik
Translator: Shmuel Himelstern
Editor: Yossi Bloch
Design: Liliya Lev Ari
Cover Design: Liliya Lev Ari

Copyright © 2014 by Contento de Semrik and Doron Almog

All rights reserved. No part of this book may be translated, reproduced, stored in a retrieval system or transmitted, in any form or by any means, electronic, photocopying, recording or otherwise, without prior permission in writing from the author and publisher.

ISBN: 978-965-550-537-5

International sole distributor:
Contento de Semrik
22 Isserles St. 67014 Tel-Aviv, Israel
Semrik10@gmail.com
www.Semrik.com

This English translation is dedicated to the memory of
Hank Greenspun
One of the many American Jews who answered the call and dedicated themselves to the creation of the State of Israel.

Table of Contents

Acknowledgements 7

Recommendations 9

Introduction by the author 21

Introduction 29

Preface 33

Chapter 1
Arms Acquisition, Given the United States Policy in the Region 41

Chapter 2
The Organizational System and its Operational Methods 59

Chapter 3
Arms Acquisition and its Contribution to the War of Independence ... 105

Chapter 4
Why was the US Potential not Utilized to the Fullest? 153

Summary 179

Bibliography 187

Appendix 193

Acknowledgements

To **Brian Greenspun** who, like his father Hank, knew how to make an ideal become reality and generously enabled the translation, editing and distribution of this book.

To **Orly Ranan** and **Hemed Publishing** House for their masterful typesetting and printing of the Hebrew addition.

To **Shmuel Himelstern** for the excellent translation from the original Hebrew manuscript.

To **Yossi Kahana**, whose dedication and determination brought to fruition another project that connects between the people of the book and the people of loving-kindness, on behalf of the disabled children of Aleh. Every effort on their behalf is a reflection of our measure of humanity and sensitivity toward the weakest members of our society.

Editor's notes:

1. This book has been translated from Hebrew. In doing so, some names may have been misspelled. The editor apologizes for any such error.

2. The footnotes in this book reference Hebrew-language sources.

Recommendations

Office of the Prime Minister 20 Heshvan, 5774
Jerusalem 24 October, 2013

My dear Doron,

I extend my heartiest congratulations on the occasion of the publication of your book, *The Commitment: A Study of the Impact of American Jews on the Establishment of the State of Israel 1945-1949*, which fascinatingly chronicles this highly significant period in the relationship between the old Yishuv settlement in the land of Israel and the Jews in America, during the years following WWII and up until the establishment of the State of Israel.

In the wake of the devastating Holocaust, which decimated one third of our people, there arose an urgent need to strengthen the emerging nascent nation, especially as the date drew near for the ruling on the establishment of the state and the future of our country. The USA government, siding on principle with the governing British Mandate, chose not to throw its weight in support of the Zionist claim for an independent homeland and for the desire of its people to enter the land freely.

There was a great need through those years – during WWII and in its aftermath, to wage an uncompromising war against the American policy which opposed a Jewish State (and I am proud to say that my father, of blessed memory, was amongst the leaders of that struggle). From the time that the official policy changed, it was deemed essential to bring in tangible aid to the Yishuv, gearing up for the fight that ultimately led to our independence.

The circumstances that transpired, as ably described in your book, meant that the Yishuv was mainly supported, both before and during the course of the War of Independence, by the Jews of the United States, guided by representatives sent from this region under the auspices of the Zionist movement. In addition to ongoing efforts to garner support within the American community for Israel's independence, there were extraordinary initiatives to obtain light and heavy artillery, to send vital supplies of fuel, foodstuff and clothing, among other essentials, and to raise donations on a large scale. All this was bolstered by the arrival of scores of volunteers arriving from overseas, who helped strengthen the defense forces in the hard battle.

In many cases, American Jews worked in the underground, clandestinely operating on behalf of their brethren here. Their incredible efforts were manifested on the ground, with the acquisition of fighting equipment, vehicles, aircraft and sea transport. All these contributed immeasurably in creating, reinforcing and strengthening the Jewish armed forces.

Doron, my dear friend, your intensive research highlights the validity of the saying: all Jews are responsible for each other. From our longstanding acquaintance over the years, I know that you have worked to implement this maxim in every phase of your life. You did that as a foot soldier and also as an acclaimed commander in the IDF – and you continue to fight today, with everything you have, on behalf of the weakest and most vulnerable segment of Israeli society.

My congratulations on your new book and with best wishes for continued success in everything you undertake.

Sincerely,
Benjamin Netanyahu
Prime Minister of the State of Israel

Dear General:

I deeply appreciate your generous gift of time and expertise yesterday in the briefing. It was insightful and inspiring to hear of your commitment to the nation of Israel and the relationship of the United States and Israel.

I hope to remain in touch. Thanks for the book about the early days of your great nation.

Gratefully,

Mike Huckabee
44th Governor of Arkansas

I just finished reading "The Commitment". Thank you for adding this important piece of information to the miracle of the founding of the State of Israel. I've seen pieces and bits of this story over the years, but this is probably the only detailed explanation.

Lester Crown
President, General Dynamics

Thank you for your kind note and your visit. Your book, COMMITMENT, will have a place of honor in our library.

Hans Levy
CEO, Environmental Company
Florida

I started reading your book at 6:30 this morning and I was mesmerized by it. I am about half way through and had to leave it to go do some work but I have to tell you I don't find it "technical" or difficult at all. On the contrary it is totally fascinating and creates wonderful historical context to think strategically about the current reality. In particular one of your opening points about the need to understand the larger context and geo political forces that inevitably shape the policies of those nations who are both your friends and your enemies. Who for example might have thought just a few years ago that the threat of Iran to contemporary gulf states could create the conditions for some sort of alliance with Israel against Iran.

I will look forward to being in touch when I finish it but I wanted to write first thing and thank you for sharing this book with me. I also must say I was deeply moved by your

Forward. You are truly a special human being.

Heather Reisman
CEO, Indigo Books

Dear Didi and Doron!

It was such a treat to see you both again last evening! I was sorry to have to remind you that you had to leave - we would have liked you to be able to stay - to visit together longer ! You are such a warm, lovely, interesting couple - we always enjoy the time we have with you - and no matter how much time transpires since we've seen each other - we can pick-up where we left off - as if we'd seen each other just last week!

Thank you so much for the copy of your book, Doron - and for your warm inscription! I started reading after you left. Your words in "Introduction by the Author" were moving - and inspiring! Larry is a slow reader - and he's very much backed-up with work reading - it's almost impossible to get him to read anything I want him to read.....So - I said: "Listen to this": and I proceeded to read it aloud to him. It wasn't easy - because I got so emotional reading it aloud that tears were streaming down my face,

Then, without my urging - he read the back cover about you, Doron, in which we both learned things about you of which we hadn't been aware.

Larry and I send our love to you both!

Larry & Barbi Weinberg
President, American Israel Public Affairs Committee (AIPAC)

General.

Wanted to thank you for your book.

Inspiring tales... It was a real pleasure meeting you.

   My best regards.

Fernando Naranjo
The Orange Group Real Estate Corp.
Miami, Florida

Besides a great presentation... I just finished General Almog's book that you so graciously provided. It was most fascinating and a real page turner.

   Thanks,

Ron Kaiser
Jewish National Fund
Western Zone
LA Office

Doron, just wanted you to know that I finally got around to reading the book you gave me on the evening of the Delaware CEO dinner.

As I expected, once I picked it up I could not put it down and was simply enthralled with the stories, the details and the names of people, some of whom I knew.

In addition, was the Hebrew version really translated by my first wife's cousin, Shmuel Himelstein of Ramot? If so, small world to be sure.

Again, thanks for giving this to me and for being who you are!

Sherwin
Sherwin Pomerantz
President, EDI Israel Investments

Dear Doron,

I just finished your book about the role of Americans in support of Israel in its early years.

This is a great story! Has anybody talked about a movie?

Eva and I have made a donation to Aleh Negev through JNF. We wish you continued success in this endeavor.

Also, we want to wish you, Didi and you family a le-shana tova.

Eva and Marv Schlanger
Marvin O. Schlanger
Chairman of the Board, CEVA Group
Member of the Board, Amerigas Partners-LP

Introduction by the author

The axiom "All of Israel is responsible for one another" expresses the commitment of Jews throughout the generations. A complete culture of bravery, faithfulness, survival, sacrifice, valor, giving, kindness, education and love is enveloped in this commitment. Indeed, it seems to be the very secret to the survival and existence of the Jewish people. In this same commitment is hidden a type of psychological, unwritten contract between a person and himself, his G-d, and his brethren. This is a contract in which a person accepts upon himself, based on his faith and deep inner feeling, sometimes after difficult internal conflict, the decision to act with determination, perseverance, and persistence on behalf of others who are in distress and in need of help. This decision embodies courage and fearlessness on behalf of someone else in need, even when it means placing one's own life in danger or performing the ultimate sacrifice to save the life of another. So we saw whole generations of Jews who sacrificed their lives, heroes like Hanna Senesh, Mordechai Anivelitz, and so many others who selflessly acted against the Nazi beast during World War II. So it was in the generation of my parents, the generation that bequeathed us the great victory of the War of Independence and the establishment of the State of Israel. And so it is in my generation who received as a precious deposit the State of Israel, the only Jewish state in the world, and is charged to continue this same commitment to ensure its existence.

During my life I accepted upon myself two commitments. The first was to fight to protect the State of Israel; the second, to fight on behalf of the weakest members of Israeli society. I accepted the first commitment during the difficult days following the Yom Kippur War in October 1973 after I found out that my beloved brother Eran, who fought as a platoon tank commander on the Golan Heights, was left behind on the battlefield to bleed to death for seven days until he was finally rescued by a unit for the rescue of the dead commanded by Professor Yaakov Neeman, then a captain. As the son of a bereaved family, I had the option of ending my combat service. Nevertheless, I decided to remain in the IDF in the most combative units, in minor and senior command positions, when all along, burning inside me was an inner promise - to do everything possible to never leave a bleeding soldier behind on the battlefield.

Three years later I found myself the first Israeli soldier to land on the grounds of Entebbe during a daring rescue operation when a handful of young, determined warriors landed in the depths of the night 4000 kilometers away from the State of Israel, killing seven terrorists and bringing back with them to Israel the Jews and Israelis that had been held hostage. The courage of the Israeli government in sending us on a mission whose success was questionable stemmed from that same commitment, the same responsibility for the fate of Jews in distress: to do everything, absolutely everything, to bring them home. A few years afterwards I participated in undercover missions to bring Ethiopian

Jews to Israel, Jews who were also in distress and danger, living under the threat of constant persecution.

This same commitment led us to land in the middle of the night in the deserts of Sudan and bring back with us on each mission about 600 completely helpless Jews who owned just the torn shirts on their backs. And this same commitment is what brought so many of my friends and fellow soldiers to give up their lives in order to secure the lives of so many others Jews, in Israel and throughout the world, in the vein of "The eternity of Israel does not lie." It is as if this commitment is engraved deep within our consciousness and has created a type of oath for uncompromising, completely dedicated action.

I accepted upon myself my second commitment after my wife and I understood that our second child, named Eran in memory of my brother Eran, would never be a regular boy. Eran was born with serious cognitive damage which resulted in a combination of autism and severe mental disabilities. We underwent a terrible crisis of the shattering of our dream of a son who would fulfill our hopes of becoming more successful and reaching greater heights than us. We had to face the reality of a son who would never marry, never have children and never realize any normative achievement according to the standards of our achieve-oriented society that waves aloft the banner of personal excellence. We swore never to be ashamed of him, never to leave him bleeding behind, to love him infinitely, and to do everything possible to create a future filled with hope for children like him in the State of Israel. On February 7, 2007, our beloved son Eran passed away from a serious illness at the young age of 23. Eran was the real professor of my life.

The child who never called me Abba is the one who taught me, more than any other person on earth, about the meaning of human sensitivity. He is the child who demonstrated for me day in and day out, hour after hour, the boundaries of human ability.

In July 2003, after nearly three years of serving as Major General of the Southern Command, dealing with more than 12,000 incidents of terror in the Gaza Strip and foiling every infiltration attempt by terrorists and would-be suicide bombers into the State of Israel, I decided to terminate my position and travel to the United States as a senior research fellow in Harvard and The Washington Institute. To many, it seemed as if I had accepted the intellectual challenge of writing strategic position papers on matters of security as a stepping stone to reaching the position of Chief of Staff of the IDF. In reality, I went to the United States to create a non-profit organization for the purpose of fundraising millions of dollars to establish a rehabilitative village for disabled children like Eran. Aleh Negev - Nahalat Eran, the village that bears the name of our son, has become a symbol in the State of Israel and the entire world; a symbol of yet another Jewish commitment, a symbol of sacrifice, giving, love, dedication and courage to do everything possible on behalf of the weakest members of society. The children of Aleh Negev-Nahalat Eran are unable to do anything for themselves. They are completely and totally dependent upon the kindness and goodwill of others. Almost like the hostages of Entebbe, only those Jews were held hostage for one week of their lives while these children bear the status of hostage their entire lives.

On July 22, 2007, Aleh Negev-Nahalat Eran was privileged to host Benjamin Netanyahu, previous Prime Minister of Israel and brother of Lieutenant Col. Yoni Netanyahu who was killed during the Entebbe rescue operation. At the conclusion of the visit I told Bibi that I was with his brother Yoni on the last day of his life, all through the long hours of the flight and until the last minutes before he fell, when I jumped first from the door of the Hercules to fulfill my mission. We flew to Entebbe to save Jewish lives in a heroic, one-time mission, and this was and remains the legacy of Yoni Netanyahu; here in Aleh Negev- Nahalat Eran we are busy saving the lives of fellow Jews every day, and this is the legacy of my brother and my son Eran. **"He who saves one life in Israel, it is as if he saved an entire world."**

Here there is constant dedication, love and sacrifice on the part of people who place their personal ego aside and instead focus on actively saving lives and doing so joyfully, even when it is difficult, overwhelming, frustrating and backbreaking.

This book is the story of the commitment accepted by a handful of brave Jews immediately following World War II. These Jews were well-established and well-known citizens of the United States of America who decided to endanger everything on behalf of a handful of other Jews who lived thousands of miles away from them, in Palestine that was ruled by the British Mandate, who had decided to establish, after 2000 years of exile which ended in the destruction of 6 million Jews, a state for the Jewish people. No one forced them to accept this commitment, which was considered in those days a foolhardy act with no chance of success. After all, what were the chances of 600,000 people living in Palestine, of which 40% were Holocaust survivors, against twenty million Arabs attacking them from all sides? Where did this small group draw the motivation and determination to smuggle in weapons, armored cars, planes, boats, ammunition and supplies? Why would wealthy, established Jews put aside their business concerns and dedicates four years to activities that were partially illegal and even conflicting the official policy of President Truman, who from December 1947 declared an embargo on sending weaponry from the U.S. to the Middle East?

This book is the **story of the generation of Hank Greenspun,** who represents this small group of American Jewry with his leadership, bravery and determination on behalf of the establishment of the State of Israel and rescuing Jews in danger, on behalf of the most meaningful values that generations of Jews were inculcated with, on behalf of that commitment that defines our essence as Jews who are responsible for one another. The charge of being "the chosen nation" is not meant to be waved about as a boastful title; rather it is a lofty mission, a difficult test, a challenge that time and again we accept with self-sacrifice in order to bestow this same privilege upon other Jews who are currently in danger and will tomorrow continue along this path as the bearers of the torch who do not forget the secret of the existence of the Jewish people:

The Commitment

Introduction

After the Six Day War, the United States became the primary outside supplier of arms to Israel, and it became so close an ally that it is difficult for an Israeli living today to understand that the attitude of the United States to the Zionist enterprise during the Israeli War of Independence (1947-1949) was far less positive.

When World War II ended, the Soviet Union changed from being an ally of the United States to being its primary rival (not its enemy). The United States accepted the obligation of being the head of the western allies in the two main world arenas against the Soviet Union and communism: in the European- Atlantic arena and in the Pacific Ocean-Japan-China arena.

Britain assumed the role of heading the pro-western alliance in the Middle East arena, confronting the Soviet Union there, and to a certain extent also in southeast Asia, dealing there with the communist rebellion in French Indochina (Vietnam, Laos, Cambodia), in Indonesia and in Malaya. Britain, under a Labour government, left India and Burma in 1947, but did not evacuate Singapore, Malaya, or northern Borneo.

In the Middle East, the British believed that only Islam and the Arabs could serve as a foundation for the desired western alliance, and regarded the Jewish Yishuv ("settlement") as a stumbling block in trying to further western interests, as it was a focus of Arab and Muslim hostility.

Had the United States policy regarding the Middle East been determined solely in terms of political considerations and American foreign policy in the world, the United States would have offered its full support to Britain, which was hostile to the Zionist enterprise, and would not have offered any help in the establishment of an independent State of Israel.

However very powerful forces in the United States served as a counterbalance to the "objective" interests of the United States in the Middle East, and influenced the granting of support to Zionism. These forces included not only the large and well-organized Jewish public, which regarded itself as the most powerful Jewish voice in the world after the Holocaust, but also the general public opinion in the country, which was very receptive to the Jewish national claim after the Holocaust, to which millions of United States soldiers in Europe had been eyewitnesses, and thereafter to what had happened in Europe.

The policy of the American president regarding the Zionist problem wavered between considerations of foreign policy as a superpower, which demanded full support for Britain, and internal considerations of elections and moral values, which pushed toward supporting the Jewish claims for free immigration into Palestine[1] and for its political independence.

---

1 Although various terms were used for the country prior to the establishment of the State of Israel, for convenience we will use "Palestine" to refer to the country before the Declaration of Independence and "the State of Israel" for the country after that event.

In these complex circumstances, it was apparent that the main source of real support for the Zionist enterprise in the United States and from the United States, prior to the War of Independence and throughout its course, was assumed by the organized Jewry of the United States, often guided by representatives sent from Palestine by the Zionist movement.

The study by Doron Almog deals in detail with the actions taken toward arms acquisition in that era in the United States, and especially in the acquisition of ships, planes, communications equipment, and modern machinery for the military industry. However we must remember that that was not the only contribution of American Jewry. Essential supplies - oil, food, clothing, etc. - arrived from the American continent, and the large financial contributions of American Jewry enabled the Zionist movement and the State of Israel to acquire sizable quantities of arms, like those purchased from Czechoslovakia, which were shipped from various places throughout the world to Israel. So too should we remember the role played by the Mahal ("overseas volunteers") from the United States and Canada in the "illegal immigration" activities in the War of Independence.

We can draw two conclusions from the events of that time, which still have bearing today: a) Israel's existential needs require it to take into account the overall strategic and political considerations of the international balance of interests; and b) the essential nature and uniqueness of the Jewish people are expressed both in Israel and in the diaspora.

Colonel (Res.) Dr. Meir Pa'il

Preface

When World War II broke out, David Ben-Gurion claimed that the realization of the aims of the Zionist movement, namely the establishment of a Jewish state, depended on the strengthening of two primary elements: the Yishuv in Palestine and world Jewry:

> From the moment that the world war broke out, I saw that history had presented us with two central tasks: the recruitment of a Jewish army during the war and the establishment of a Jewish state immediately after the war ... However it was clear to me that the only forces upon which we could rely under any circumstances were two: the Jewish Yishuv in Palestine and world Jewry, and first and foremost American Jewry, and only if we were able to recruit these two forces for our central aims at this decisive time, could we possibly overcome those forces which stood in our way and thus attain our desired aim.[2]

---

2   See: David Ben-Gurion, "BaDerekh LeTzava UleMedinat Yisrael" (On the Way to an Army and to the State of Israel), a series of articles published in Davar in the years 1963-4. From Article 22, which was published on December 27, 1963 (henceforth: "On the Way").

About six weeks after the publication of the "White Paper" (which severely curtailed Jewish immigration to Palestine) in May 1939, Ben-Gurion stressed in a speech before the Zionist Executive the path that would lead to the strengthening of the Yishuv in Palestine:

> Our future in Palestine depends on two things: immigration by every means, and the establishment of a Jewish army by every means – by every legal way, if that is possible, and by every illegal way which we can establish[3].

At the end of September 1940, just before he left from London for New York, Ben-Gurion recognized the centrality of the United States as a superpower and the possibilities inherent in American Jewry as a central pillar in bringing about the fulfillment of Zionism:

> It became clear to me that our decisive battleground - outside Palestine itself - is not in England, but in the United States, and there is no more effective and supportive a lever than American Jewry and the Zionist movement in America, where the fate of the democratic world possibly lies. In spite of the weakness of this Jewry, I was sure that it would not disappoint us, just as I believed that the United States would not remain neutral for an extended time period in the world struggle, where at this time the entire fate of the honor of all of mankind lies[4].

The surrender of Japan on August 14, 1945, which brought about the conclusion of World War II, demonstrated the military superiority of the United States and its status as the mightiest industrial power in

---

3   Ibid. Article 18, November 29, 1963.
4   Ibid. Article 23, January 4, 1964.

the world. Between July 1, 1940 and September 30, 1944, the American industrial output included about 70,000 tanks and 230,000 planes of various types, along with their armaments. This was in addition to the military materièl supplied to about11,500,000 American enlisted men. In order to make up for the losses caused by the sinking of ships by the Germans, the United States ports in 1943 alone built an average of three ships a day[5]!

Thus World War II transformed the United States into the largest arms manufacturer in the world. Understandably, the end of the war brought about a drastic decrease in the arms manufacture in the country, and the War Assets Administration decided to set up sales warehouses which would offer purchasing agents throughout the world military equipment of all kinds.

In very stark contrast to the mighty American power, the Jews of the world were in deep shock after having learned of the Holocaust of European Jewry. The murder of six million Jews intensified the demands of the Zionist movement. The survivors of the Nazi camps were not only living witnesses to what had occurred, but also created an immediate need to solve this humanitarian problem. In that situation, it was only natural that American Jews had a deep sense of guilt. The feeling that they had not done enough to exert pressure on the Roosevelt administration to implement rescue efforts and to help European Jewry caused them to feel weighed down by guilt, and this was expressed, from 1945 on, by determined activities to establish a Jewish state in Palestine. Politically, the peak of this activity was expressed in the UN resolution of November 29, 1947, on the

---

[5] See: V.A. Caldwell and A.H. Merrill, Korot HaOlam (History of the World), edited by Michael Ziv, Masada, Tel Aviv, 19068, pp. 861-862.

establishment of two independent states in Palestine, an Arab state and a Jewish state. The granting of international recognition of the demand for Jewish sovereignty in Palestine was without a doubt a highly significant turning point in the history of the Jewish people. Militarily, this activity focused on the formation of an underground organization which dealt - generally secretly, and in many cases against United States law - in acquiring military materièl, machinery, airplanes and ships, which were a significant contribution to the "illegal" immigration efforts and in strengthening the Hebrew army in the State of Israel once it had been established, in the most difficult time of the War of Independence[6].

It is the aim of this book to examine the following questions:

a. How did the Jewish underground in the United States, which dealt with acquisitions, organize and how did it act? To what extent was it the initiator of its actions and to what extent was it used as a "lever"? What were the differences between the acquisition activities of the Haganah and those of Etzel?

b. What was the total materièl contribution of the acquisition activities in the United States and to what extent did it affect the struggle and the victory in the War of Independence?

c. Was the potential granted by the United States to the acquisition activities and to the formation of the Jewish army utilized properly? Could not the five million[7] Jews of the United States have contributed

---

[6] See: David Ben-Gurion, "**MiHazon LeMedinah ad Milhemet HaKomemiyut**" (From the Vision of a State until the War of Independence), in **Toledot Milhemet HaKomemiyut (The History of the War of Independence)**, Ma'arakhot,Tel Aviv, July 1968, pp. 23-27.

[7] See: Marshall Sklar, **Yehudei Artzot HaBrit (The Jews of the United States)**, Am Oved, Tel Aviv, 1972, p. 38.

more than they actually contributed? What were the limitations to their activities in the United States, and how did they deal with them?

d. What is the in-depth significance of the acquisition activities in the United States as a collective act of the American Jews for the establishment and strengthening of the State of Israel in the circumstances as they were?

e. The decision by the Jewish Agency Executive, after the 22nd Zionist Congress of December 1946, to make Ben-Gurion the chairman of the administration and the head of the defense department[8] formally made him the person who assumed the greatest responsibility for the deeds and failures of the defense system. How can one assess the degree of success of Ben-Gurion in particular, and of the defense system in general, in translating that which he had said at the end of the 1930s and the beginning of the 1940s into actual actions in the United States in the years 1945 to 1949? Why wasn't the World War II period utilized for a more massive arms acquisition in the United States? Were five crucial years "wasted"?

The primary limitation of this study stems from the fact that most of the archival material related to the actions of the Jews of the United States for arms acquisition is to be found in that country, and at this time it is inaccessible. The primary sources of this study are thus the archival material available in Israel, which reflects the acquisition activities

---

8 See: "HaDiyun HaMedini BaKongress Ha'Chaf Bet" (The Political Discussion at the 22nd Congress), **Sefer Toledot HaHaganah (The Book of the History of the Haganah)**, chief ed. Benzion Dinur, Vol. 3: MiMa'avak LeMilhamah From Struggle to War), Part II, Am Oved, Tel Aviv, 1972, pp. 832-833.

from the perspective of the Haganah emissaries. In addition, there are autobiographical accounts by some of the individuals involved in the acquisition, personal interviews with them, and newspaper accounts.

Chapter 1:

Arms Acquisition, Given the United States Policy in the Region

A Policy Devoid of Any Commitment to the Establishment of a Jewish State

In 1917, President Woodrow Wilson supported the Balfour Declaration and declared that its approach regarding the Palestine problem was acceptable to the United States. Nevertheless, at the same time, the United States was of the opinion that the major role to be played in the Middle East should be that of Britain and France. In spite of its involvement in the peace conference held in Paris in March 1919, and in spite of the King-Crane commission, in the period between the two world wars the United States adopted a position of non-intervention in political and strategic issues in the Middle East. As opposed to this, it expanded its involvement in the region commercially and economically, especially in the realm of oil. Only on the Palestinian issue did the United States' interest approach a political obligation, but here too it limited itself to expressing vague support for the establishment of a Jewish national home in Palestine. In truth, up to World War II the United States did not take any concrete steps in this regard[9].

World War II brought about a massive presence of the United States in the Middle East, and as a result its strategic involvement in the region, while formulating its policies, both politically and in terms of defense. Bases were set up in the region, along with supply depots and transportation and communication centers, and American soldiers were stationed in these. Military bases were established in Libya and Saudi Arabia, while economic and technical aid was granted to Turkey, Iran, and other countries. During World War II, the Middle East was the link which connected the United States and the Soviet Union in implementing aid to the Soviets, by means of a route which passed through the Persian Gulf and Iran. In spite of that fact, Britain continued to carry the bulk of responsibility for the Middle East, including those areas which involved military involvement, such as the Middle East supply center[10].

The focus of Zionist activity was transferred from London to the United States. The Biltmore Conference, which convened in New York in May 1942, marked a highly significant turning point in the

---

9 See: Bernard Reich and Arnold Gutfeld, Artzot HaBrit VeHaSikhsukh HaYisraeli- Aravi (The United States and the Israeli-Arab Dispute) (henceforth: The United States and the Israeli-Arab Dispute), Ma'arakhot, Tel Aviv, 1977, pp. 11-12.

10 Ibid. pp. 13-14.

Zionist activity in this country, even though the Biltmore Program had very little influence on the American government and its Middle East policy. The Conference symbolized the radicalization of the Zionist Organization as a result of the war and the losses suffered by the Jewish People, and was evidenced by the demand to establish a Jewish state immediately. In the years after the Conference, the Zionists in the United States invested great efforts in attempting to have the American government support the idea of the establishment of a Jewish state in Palestine[11].

The war highlighted the strategic value of the region. The growing interest of the United States in the region's resources, especially its oil, added to its importance.

The emergence of the United States after the war as a global force and a superpower increased its need to reformulate a comprehensive policy in regard to the Middle East. In spite of this, it entered the postwar era without any clearly defined plan regarding the region, and was guided primarily by the need to prevent a local dispute from deteriorating into a situation which would force the superpowers into a world war. Thus, for example, in September 1946, Loy

Henderson - director of the State Department's Near East Agency at that time made the following proposal regarding the United States policy in the Middle East:

The primary aim of the United States in the Middle East and the Near East is to prevent the development of rivalries and conflicting interests in this region from becoming openly hostile acts, which are liable to provoke a third world war ... Until such time as all the

---
11 See: Walter (Ze'ev) Lacquer, Toledot HaTziyonut (History of Zionism), Schocken: Jerusalem and Tel Aviv, 1974, pp. 429-431.

nations of the Middle East and the Near East are stable politically and economically, and until their governments are stable and capable of maintaining internal order and of taking measures which will improve the standard of living of their populations, the Middle East and the Near East will continue to be a temptation to those powers which are outside the region. As long as that temptation exists, the danger will continue that this dispute can ignite a war[12].

The American Secretary of State, John Foster Dulles, coined the phrase, "the northern tier," referring to those countries along the northern edge of the Middle East and on the southern border of the Soviet Union, countries which feared "the danger of Soviet communism," and because of this fear expressed "a great desire to establish a joint defense system.[13]"

This policy was first implemented in regard to Iran, Turkey, and Greece: the Truman Doctrine of March 1947 promised financial and economic aid to Greece and Turkey in order to help them cope with aggressive and subversive forces. This was the first significant United States policy in the Middle East, and by it the United States replaced Britain, which had been the traditional patron of these states.

In spite of the Truman Doctrine, the United States did not formulate a comprehensive policy toward the other countries of the Middle East, including Palestine. In regard to Palestine, the United States continued to hold the view that the primary responsibility for stability in the region had to remain with Britain. Its involvement in regard to Palestinian affairs in the years after World War II was concentrated

---

12 See: Middle East Journal, 1 January, 1947, p. 85.
13 Ibid. Note 8, p. 15; similarly, pp. 112-120.

primarily on the problem of the emigration from Europe of the Jews who had survived the Holocaust. However, its concern was primarily humanitarian, and it sought to deal only with this aspect, while leaving the political and security problems in British hands. Truman believed that the best solution to the humanitarian problem was to permit the "Displaced Persons" to immigrate to Palestine, and his policy was also based on the need to fulfill the promises regarding the establishment of a Jewish national home in Palestine:

> I wished to help in the realization of the undertaking of the Balfour Declaration, and of the saving of at least a part of the victims of the Nazis. I did not undertake to support a state in Palestine or a specified timetable for its realization. The American policy was meant to achieve, by peaceful means, the establishment of the promised Jewish homeland, and to make it easier for the displaced Jews in Europe to enter it[14].

On August 31, 1945, Truman wrote to the British Prime Minister, Clement Atlee, and implored him to permit the emigration of 100,000 displaced Jews from Europe to Palestine[15]. His request was made based on a report by Earl Harrison regarding the condition in June-July 1945 of those who had survived the Holocaust[16]. Truman's request negated the provisions of the "White Paper," and therefore Britain proposed

---

14 See: Harry S. Truman, "Leidat Yisrael," Shnot Masa VeTohelet ("The Birth of Israel of Israel," Years of Trial and Hope), Vol. 2, Ayanot, Tel Aviv, 1956, p. 162 (henceforth: Years of Trial and Hope).
15 Foreign Relations of the United States, Diplomatic Papers, 1945, Washington 1966, Vol. VIII, pp. 737-739.
16 See: Zevi Ganim, "HaMa'avak HaMedini Erev Hakamat HaMedinah" (The Political Struggle Prior to the Establishment of the State), in Sekirah Hodshit (Monthly Review); henceforth: The Political Struggle Prior to the Establishment of the State), April 1975, p. 8; similarly, Years of Trial and Hope, p. 142.

that a joint investigative committee be formed to clarify the issue of Palestine and the Displaced Persons in Palestine. The committee was established in November 1945, and in its conclusions, which were presented in April 1946, it proposed, among others, that 100,000 Jews be permitted to enter Palestine. At the same time, it emphasized that the establishment of an independent state was liable to launch a civil war.

The danger of a war developing between the Jews and the Arabs was regarded by Truman as "a serious threat to world peace.[17]" After returning from the Potsdam Conference in August 1945, he had announced that the Jewish State could only arise through peaceful means, through negotiations with the British and the Arabs. "I have no desire to send half a million American soldiers to bring peace to Palestine.[18]"

This statement proves that Truman had been influenced by the basically anti-Zionist approach of the American State Department and of the British Foreign Office, both of which believed that a Jewish state in Palestine could only be established and continue to exist by means of British or American military intervention, which would force such a state upon the Arabs. Such a step was liable to inflame the Arab and Muslim world against the United States, and would thus endanger the United States' interests in the Middle East. It is also possible that Truman was influenced by the "American Council for Judaism," which claimed that a Jewish state would be a theocratic one which would adversely discriminate against its non-Jewish residents. A state

---

17 See: Years of Trial and Hope, p. 165.
18 See: The Political Struggle Prior to the Establishment of the State, p. 8.

such as that would be against the United States' view regarding the separation of church and state[19].

All of this can explain the character of the conclusions of the Anglo-American committee on the one hand, and Truman's insistence on the immigration of 100,000 Displaced Persons to Palestine on the other. Britain was afraid that the Arab opposition to the immigration of 100,000 Jews would provoke riots not only in Palestine, but also in a number of Arab and Muslim countries. On the other hand, Britain was afraid of a break with President Truman, and it therefore proposed a compromise: the establishment of a second Anglo-American committee. Thus the "Morrison-Grady plan" was born in July 1946[20].

The conclusions of this second committee, which proposed that the country be divided into four regions based on the principle of federation, with Britain in control of security, external affairs, and taxes, were rejected by Truman on August 12, 1946, in a telegram to Atlee[21]. After the failure of the second London conference, and with it another plan, the "Bevin Plan," Britain transferred the Palestine problem to the UN in the spring of 1947.

The UNSCOP Commission submitted its proposals regarding the "Partition Plan" to the UN on November 29, 1947. The proposal was approved by the General Assembly by a vote of 33 to 13, with 10 abstentions. The decision by the United States to support partition was the most important political decision of that time in regard to Palestine and the future of the State of Israel. However, this proposal, as well, was not the result of a new policy of the United States, but was

---

19 Ibid. p. 8. Dr. Meir Pa'il states that in these years the United States had a vital interest in having Britain remain in the Middle East, and to continue to be a key power in organizing the entire region - from central Asia through the eastern Mediterranean - facing off against the Soviet Union.
20 Ibid. p. 11.
21 Ibid. p. 12.

based primarily on the desire to solve the humanitarian problem of the Displaced Persons. Basic policy differences between Loy Henderson, who was one of the leaders of those opposed to the Partition Plan, and its supporters, continued to characterize the Truman administration throughout the Israeli War of Independence, and only with that background can one understand the inconsistency of the American policy regarding the realization of the Zionist dream.

But six days after the United States supported the Partition Plan, it placed an arms embargo on the region in an effort to prevent an armed conflict. Thus, even if such a conflict were to break out, the embargo would limits its dimensions and the weapons used in the conflict. On December 5, 1947, the State Department imposed an embargo on the shipment of arms to the region in dispute. This was to encompass all materièl outside the United States as well, including the transfer or shifting of arms and ammunition of the Lend-Lease program, or the sale of surplus arms and ammunition of the United States[22].

The increased hostilities between the Arabs and the Jews in the period from November 1947 to May 1948 highlighted the hesitation of the administration and the internal differences within it, and was evidence of the lack of any strong commitment within it to the establishment of a Jewish state. Truman's comments emphasized the dilemma. As he wrote in his memoirs in regard to Palestine, the Army kept emphasizing two matters: the inability of the United States to send troops to the region should it goes up in flames, and the oil reserves of the Middle East. Secretary of Defense Forrestal discussed with Truman, on a number of occasions, the danger should hostile

---

22 The United States and the Israeli-Arab Dispute, p. 22, Note 3.

Arab nations refuse to supply the United States with oil from their reserves. The Middle East experts of the State Department were almost unanimously opposed to the idea of a Jewish state. They explained their stand as follows: Britain had forged relationships in the area by fostering friendship with the Arabs. Now that it appeared that Britain was unable to continue in this path, the United States should replace it, and it should do so exactly in the way that Britain had acted. If the United States angered the Arabs, they would move over to the Soviet bloc. Truman claimed that he had never felt that these arguments by the diplomats were persuasive. He added that, in this dispute between the White House and the State Department in regard to Palestine, there had never been any doubt as to who had the final say and whose policy would be implemented. The argument was about the timing but never about whether the state should be established[23].

UNSCOP - the United Nations Special Commission on Palestine - reported to the UN Security Council that the termination of the British mandate over Palestine on May 14, 1948 would bring about violence and anarchy unless the UN would supply the force necessary to enforce the partition. Britain refused to take part in any such operation and the United States did not want to participate in any such force. At the same time, the United States objected to the Soviet Union's participation in any such force. Other countries proposed that the termination of the Mandate be delayed until such time as a solution could be found to

---

[23] See: Years of Trial and Hope, p. 167. According to Dr. Meir Pa'il, the primary consideration of the United States' policy in the region was the formation of an anti-Soviet bloc. To accomplish this, the United States needed the support of Britain and of the Arab world. However, because of internal pressures, (the claims of the Jews and their supporters, and the refusal of the United States to accept the surviving remnant of the Jewish people of Europe in its borders) the President was unable to act totally according to its own interests.

this problem. The United States appeared to be wavering as to what course of action should be taken.

This indecision stemmed from the hesitation of the Departments of State and of Defense and their opposition to the line adopted by President Truman.

On February 24, 1948, the representative of the United States to the UN, Warren Austen, informed the Security Council that his country did not believe that it was possible to use force to enforce the new partition resolution. On March 19, 1948, Austen declared that since at that time it was impossible to implement the partition resolution by peaceful means, the United States was in favor of a temporary trusteeship of the UN over Palestine, as an emergency means, whose purpose was to ensure public order and not as a replacement of partition. At the same time, many regarded this proposal as an American retreat from the partition plan. The Arabs, too, were against the trusteeship proposal, because they thought that it was too generous to the Zionists. In the end, the UN General Assembly at Lake Success rejected the trusteeship plan, due to a failure of broad support[24].

On May 14, while the UN was deliberating about Palestine, Britain terminated its mandate and in Tel Aviv the State of Israel was proclaimed. And as Truman wrote in his memoirs, eleven minutes after the State of Israel was proclaimed, his press secretary announced that the United States recognized *de facto* the provisional government of Israel[25].

---

24 See: Ze'ev Schiff, "HaUmot HeMe'uhadot Mitvakhot" (The United Nations Argue), Shloshet Yamim - 12, 13, 14 BeMai 1948 (Three Days - 12, 13, 14 May 1948), Am Oved, Tel Aviv, 1959, pp. 34-35.
25 See: Years of Trial and Hope, p. 169. Dr. Meir Pa'il explains that Truman's reasons for doing so were: a) internal pressures with Jewish backing; b) the fear that the Soviet Union would be the only country to aid Israel and that if Israel survived the Soviet Union would have a bridgehead in the area.On the other hand, if Israel fell the United States president would be blamed for having abandoned it.

Following the Declaration of Independence and the exit of the British from Palestine, the armies of Egypt, Jordan, Syria, Lebanon and Iraq attacked the State of Israel. Throughout the war, the United States refrained from intervening. It supported the mediating efforts of the UN to solve the problem, and already on May 14, 1948 it voted for the resolution of the General Assembly to appoint a mediator to deal with the issue. On December 1948 11, the United States supported a resolution of the General Assembly of the UN to establish a reconciliation commission for Palestine, where a United States delegate would be a member. It also supported the effort to achieve ceasefires and to validate that these were indeed in effect under the supervision of a UN body (UNTSO - United Nations Truce Supervision Organization) and on January 31, 1949, it granted Israel *de jure* recognition[26].

The embargo decision of December 1947, the policy of non-intervention in the struggle of the State of Israel in the War of Independence, and the contradiction between the desire to help in solving the problem of the Holocaust refugees and the lack of decisiveness and of any feeling of compulsion to establish the State of Israel was a major influence on the readiness of the Jews of the United States to involve themselves in underground activities for the "state in the making," and also influenced the arms acquisition activities in this country at the time.

---

26 Ibid.p. 170.

The Advantages and Limitations of the Arms Acquisition Activities

The Advantages

The United States, as a pluralistic country which encourages private investment and initiative, created the possibility of the establishment of fictitious companies, which were, in practice, affiliated with real companies of people of means who supported the Zionist effort, but were in reality no more than fronts for illegal acquisition activities[27].

The largest Jewish concentration in the world (with about 5 million souls) was in the United States, and this, coupled with public opinion which was sympathetic with the Zionist struggle, made it possible to undertake voluntary activities on a wide scale, beginning with raising money and items which were not included in the embargo, through the recruitment of hundreds of actual volunteers. The United States was not only the largest arms warehouse in the world, but was also the world leader in industrial development and technological progress. Access was freely available to advanced information, in most cases completely openly, through professional journals, catalogs, and exchanges of letters with industrial corporations and the appropriate government departments. The presence in this country of the best brains related to the development of advanced technologies was also a source for extracting information.

During World War II, there were many Jewish enlisted men and officers in the United States army. They amassed a great deal of military experience, and were willing to help in establishing a Jewish

---

27 Sa'adiah Gelb - interview, Rehovot, May 22, 1985 (I have the recorded tapes.)

army in Palestine, both in terms of active involvement and in offering advice, training, and organization. The Jewish youth movements - HaBonim, HaShomer HaTza'ir, Bnei Akiva, and HeHalutz - were willing to make available dozens of youths to help in arms acquisitions - both legal and illegal - for the struggle in Palestine. Wealthy Jews, both Zionist and non-Zionist, were prepared to offer a sizable part of their assets, resources, and energy to help in organizing underground illegal activities, such as crating and storing military equipment meant for Palestine.

It would thus appear that the best chance of success of such acquisitions should have been in the United States: the world storehouse of arms, superior technology, a concentration of brainpower, free access to information, favorable public opinion, economic wealth, a democratic regime, and unlimited resources. However, even though there was no other country which offered all these conditions, the United States was not - as one might have imagined - in first place in supplying arms for the establishment of the Jewish army; the majority of acquisitions were in Europe - illegally. The policies of the American administration were very influential in the final results.

The Limitations

In 1794, the United States' "Neutrality Law" was passed, which stated that if anyone is enlisted or hires himself out or leaves the jurisdictional area of the United States in order to serve any foreign ruler or country, he has violated the law. Later, the federal law determined the punishment in the event of a conviction: a fine of up to a thousand dollars or three years of incarceration or both punishments together[28].

The key words in the American neutrality law, "to hire" and "to employ," refer to the territorial area of the United States.

All the Jews and non-Jews who were involved in the arms acquisition thus walked a very thin line. The problem became much worse after the Declaration of the State, when hundreds of volunteers wanted to be actively involved in the struggle of the young state. The United States administration was liable to convict volunteers, as it had done previously in other cases and in other wars; however, when public opinion disagrees with the over-rigorous interpretation of the neutralism law, no jury will convict.

As long as the British mandate was still in effect in Palestine, the United States policy could not permit the acquisition of military equipment which could be used by the Jewish Yishuv in its struggle against the British or the Arabs. The British mandate forbade anyone from owning arms or from bringing any into the country, and the United States, as an ally of Britain which identified with the basic principles of British policy, could not grant legitimation to arms acquisition which was against British policy. The embargo of December 1947 was primarily a declared continuation of that policy.

On March 26, 1948 President Truman issued his Directive 2776, which expanded the "weapons list," the arms or military equipment which would need a special license by the State Department before being exported. The four main changes in the list extended it to

---

28 See: Leonard Slater, HaNe'emanim: Mosdot HaRekhesh BeTaShaKH (The Trustees: the Acquisition Institutions in 5708 (1948), Ma'arakhot, Tel Aviv, 1971 (Henceforth: The Trustees), p. 184.

all civilian aircraft, all aircraft parts and equipment, equipment for calibrating firing ranges and distances, and certain military electronic items, including radar[29]. Up to that point, licenses to export military aircraft could only be granted after a year's delay. From now on this law was extended to civilian aircraft as well, and these needed the approval of the State Department's arms supervision authority, and it even applied to friendly nations on the American continent, such as Panama.

This directive was supposed to go into effect on April 15, 1948. The approaching termination of the British mandate in Palestine thus brought about a hardening of the military export policy of the United States.

The limitations in terms of acquiring and exporting military equipment, along with civilian equipment which could be used for military purposes, were the result of the American policy in regard to Palestine. These limitations were what brought the underground organization of arms purchases and shipment, with the maximal amount of compartmentalization, in order to carry out the illegal acquisition of armaments. The United States, as a law-abiding and sophisticated country, which operates supervisory commands, police, and spies, now had to contend with underground activity meant to smuggle out military equipment in illegal ways.

The end of the British mandate in Palestine also marked the end of the first stage in Israel's War of Independence - the stage of defending the different settlements and the main highways. As Ben-Gurion put it:

The transition from the defense of different locations to defense of the country also means the adoption of new tools. Rifles, mortars, machine

---

[29] Ibid. p. 216 (emphasis mine).

guns, and hand grenades are no longer enough for us. We need heavy machines, cannon and fighter planes, bombers and military vehicles, and naval vessels in the sea ... No longer local defense but national; not static defense, but dynamic[30].

The American embargo did indeed apply to both the Arabs and the Jews, but the Arab states already had arms by the time the embargo went into effect: they had bought surplus United States arms for thirty-seven million dollars through the United States war surplus sales organization, and had also been equipped by Britain, which had not stopped supplying them. The British did not follow in the footsteps of the Americans, and justified their actions as being based on "contractual obligations" toward the Arab states[31].

As opposed to expectations, the United States did not take any further steps after its vote in favor of partitioning the land, and did not sell the Jewish state the arms it needed to defend its nascent sovereignty. On the contrary: it prevented the Jews from receiving arms. This was a terrible blow, which crushed all the hopes and plans, and required the Jewish leadership to come to a most cruel conclusion: that in spite of the might of the United States, it was impossible to reach any large-scale agreement with it regarding arms acquisition, one which might supply the new state with its most immediate needs in heavy artillery, cannon, tanks, armored vehicles, an air force and a navy. The different organizations involved in arms acquisition - starting with the leadership of the Yishuv in Palestine, through the official Jewish organizations in the United States and up to the arms acquisition

---

30 See: David Ben-Gurion, BeHilahem Yisrael (When Israel Fought), Mapai (the Israel Labor Party), Second Edition, Tel Aviv, 1951, pp. 34-35.
31 See: The Trustees, p. 114.

apparatuses in that country - thus found themselves having to work against American law.

The leadership of US Jewry with President Truman

(from left to right: President Truman, Dr. Emmanuel Neuman, Dr. Abba Hillel Silver)

Chapter 2:

The Organizational System and its Operational Methods

The Etzel and the Haganah in the United States during World War II

World War II was the primary motivator for the establishment of the action centers of Etzel and the Haganah in the United States. The primary importance of these centers lay in the fact that they carried within themselves the embryo of the organizational structure of the arms acquisitions which were later carried out after the war.

The Etzel

The first person sent to the United States, at the end of 1939, was Haim Lubinski, accompanied by Colonel Paterson, on behalf of the New Zionist Organization. They were followed by Hillel Kook in July 1940,

Alexander Rafaeli, Aryeh Ben-Eliezer, and Yitzhak Ben-Ami (Rosen). Immediately after they arrived, they set up the American Friends of Jewish Palestine organization[32], and embarked on an open campaign to enlist American public opinion to support the illegal immigration they were organizing and a public campaign to finance this immigration. The American Friends helped to finance a ship named the Skaria, which reached the shores of Palestine in the spring of 1940, with 2300 refugees on its deck. The Zionist organizations in the United States opposed the methods adopted by the American Friends. A letter sent on March 1, 1940 by the deputy director of the United Jewish Appeal, Henry Montor, to Rabbi B. Rabinowitz expressed this opposition most vehemently, and this may help in understanding the strained relationship which would later develop between the Etzel emissaries and the official Zionist institutions[33].

The arrival of Ze'ev Jabotinski in the United States in March 1940 brought about an expansion of the activities of Etzel, primarily in working at enlisting public opinion to support the establishment of a Jewish army. The American Friends turned to the British government, through Britain's ambassador to the United States, to request that it recognize Etzel as a legal organization whose aim was to protect Palestine. The British government replied on June 19, 1940 that it could not offer such recognition as Etzel was an illegal organization which

---

32 See: Eli Tavin, HaHazit HaSheniyah (The Second Front), Ron, Tel Aviv, 1973, p. 29 (the book is based on the author's doctoral dissertation, as approved by the Hebrew University of Jerusalem); henceforth: HaHazit HaSheniyah. So too, see: David Niv, Ma'arakhot HaIrgun HaTzeva'i HaLe'umi, Hafuga VeKonenut 1940-1944 (Campaigns of the Irgun - Truce and Preparedness 1940-1944), Part III, Mossad Klausner, Tel Aviv, 1967 (henceforth: "Ma'arakhot HaIrgun).

33 Ibid. p. 40, Note 30.

was involved in terror in Palestine[34]. Jabotinski's death in August 1940 did not slow down the pace of the expansion of the movement's activities. Aharon Zevi Propes, the Betar commander in the United States, came up with the idea of the "League of Jewish Aviation." The plan was carried into effect in February 1941, with a flying school named after Jabotinski in Rockaway, New York. This school trained about fifty Jewish pilots, who fought in Germany in the United States air force[35].

On December 4, 1941 the official announcement was made in Washington about the establishment of the Committee for a Hebrew Army, headed by the author Pierre van Paassen and administered by Hillel Kook, who called himself Peter Bergson. It was the task of this committee to act toward the establishment of an army of 200,000 Jews from Palestine and other places. These would fight under the Supreme Commander of the Allies, and after the victory over Hitler they would want that army to return to Jerusalem. They sought a Jewish government to be established in Jerusalem, which would guarantee freedom and equal rights for every Muslim and Christian[36]. In order to stir up public opinion, the members of the committee used unrestrained publicity methods, which, among others, included full-page advertisements in the leading daily American newspapers.

The year 1942 was the year of the main struggle for the establishment of a Jewish army. The primary activists in the committee were Hillel

---

34 Ibid. p. Note 30.
35 Avigdor Shachan, "Pe'ilut Te'ufatit LeMa'an HaYishuv BeEretz Yisrael" (Aviational Activity for the Yishuv in Palestine), Kanfei Nitzahon (Wings of Victory), Am Hasefer, Tel Aviv, 1966, pp. 42-45.
36 From a speech by Harden Soref, president of the Carnegie Institute, as quoted in HaHazit HaSheniyah, p.30

Kook, Paterson, Meir Grossman, Ari Jabotinski, Eliahu ben-Horin, and Benzion Netanyahu. In spite of the friction between the Jewish Agency and the Committee, there is no doubt that the establishment of the Jewish Brigade was due to both of their efforts. In 1943, after the details of the Jewish annihilation had become known, the Committee began to focus its effort on saving the remaining Jews of Europe. Its activities were expanded by the establishment of the "Emergency Committee to Save the Jewish People in Europe."

The war against Britain which the Etzel had declared in January 1944 caused the emissaries of the organization in the United States to establish the "Hebrew Committee for National Liberation." On July 7, the members of the committee were registered with the State Department, in accordance with United States law, as agents of the Hebrew nation (see Appendix A). Leading the committee were Hillel Kook (Peter Bergson) as chairman, Samuel Merlin as general secretary, and T. Ben-Nahum as treasurer. Other members were Ari Jabotinski, Prof. Dlugosh and Y. Halperin. The aims of the committee were: to save the Jews from the Nazi clutches; to establish a Hebrew army which would help the Allies in the struggle against the Nazis; to conduct a major propaganda campaign for armed rebellion against the British mandate in accordance with Etzel's pronouncement; and to establish a Hebrew state in Palestine[37].

The methods used by Kook and his colleagues were in most cases provocative and direct. There is no doubt that these methods attracted a great deal of interest and brought to the attention of the American public and the administration the death cries of the European Jews, who were being murdered. On the other hand, these actions severely handicapped any attempts to work clandestinely, something which is

---

37 Ibid. pp. 32-34, 269.

necessary when one carries out illegal acts. The methods used by Etzel in the United States in the war period and the cause of friction between it and the Zionist institutions are important for one to understand the limits of its undercover work and the poor results which it showed in arms acquisition after the war.

The Haganah

While the actions of Etzel were not dependent on the position adopted by the official Zionist institutions in the United States, the actions of the Haganah in the war years took into account the position of these institutions although it did not function in coordination with them, and the cooperation was based on their respective administrative and logistical competencies.

From 1939, Israel Meriminski worked in the United States as an emissary of the fundraising appeal on behalf of the Executive of the Histadrut. He also worked to strengthen the ties and to coordinate with the Zionist movements - HeHalutz, HaShomer, HaBonim, and task-oriented organizations on the one hand, and to foster personal ties with American politicians and administration officials on the other. Under him was a group of Haganah personnel whose head was Yosef Yizre'eli. Yizre'eli arrived in the United States together with Shalom Worm, Moshe Levin, and Ovadiah Yosselovitz[38].

Yosef Yizre'eli was the one who came up with the idea of establishing a commercial airline in Palestine, whose pilots would be trained in the United States and whose existence would enhance the security of the Yishuv in Palestine. The idea was presented to the heads of HeHalutz, and they put it into practice by establishing a flight school on the

---

38 See: Sa'adiah Gelb, interview, Rehovot, May 22, 1985.

HeHalutz farm in Heights Town, New Jersey. The flying school trained about twenty pilots, many of whom fought later in the British and American armies, and a number of whom were among the founders of the Israel Air Force. Among the latter were Major General Aharon Remez, the first commander of the Israel Air Force, Colonel Hyman Shamir, the vice-commander of the Air Force at its founding and consolidation, and Pinhas (Percy) Tolchinski, the commander of the Galilee squadron of the Air Service[39].

Yosef Yizre'eli opened a radio station in New York and used a recruiting system to utilize the manpower of the Zionist movement for Haganah projects. His methods and those of Meriminski can be regarded as embryonic of the Haganah activity in the years between 1945 and 1949, where those involved in political activities acted openly and in ways which were reminiscent of those of the Kook group, whereas those involved in arms procurement acted secretly, using various action groups which were compartmentalized one from the other.

The activities of the Haganah members in the United States throughout World War II were influenced by the visits of two important people to the United States: Moshe Sharett (Shertok) and Reuven Shiloah (Zaslani). The former dealt with the political realm while the latter was more involved with intelligence. Zaslani began to conduct meetings in order to explain the needs of the Haganah in Palestine. Most of his approaches to the official Zionist bodies were turned down, due to the hints he dropped about involvement in secret and illegal activities in order to acquire weaponry and to establish a Jewish army in Palestine. At the beginning of 1945 Zaslani even sent a secret memo to Ben-

---

39 See: Kanfei Nitzahon, pp. 46-47; similarly, Ma'arkhot HaIrgun HaTzeva'i HaLe'umi (The Campaigns of the National Military Organization = Irgun), pp. 113-114.

Gurion, who was then the head of the Jewish Agency, and reported that in everything related to his special activities, one could not rely on official Zionist organizations in the United States[40].

In May and June, 1945, Ben-Gurion was in London, trying to ascertain the political policies of Britain regarding Palestine after the war was over. The end of the war offered the perfect opportunity to equip the Haganah with a modern military infrastructure. Moshe Shertok and Moshe Sneh, head of the Haganah command at the time, spurred Ben-Gurion on in that direction. In a message which reached him in London, they informed him that "Sneh proposes that Avi Amos [Ben-Gurion's underground code name] and Eliezer [Kaplan] should work in America to create a defense fund of between 5 and 10 million dollars for the defense of the Yishuv should it be attacked ... Moshe concurs with this proposal.[41]"

The commander of the Air Force, Aharon Remez (second from right) **and his deputy, Hyman Shamir** (second from left)

---

40 See: The Trustees, p. 72.
41 See: Michael Bar-Zohar, "Mivrak MeiAvi Amos" (A Telegram from Avi Amos), Ben-Gurion, Am Oved, Tel Aviv, 1975, Vol. I, p. 514.

Ben-Gurion's arrival in the United States at the end of June 1945 caused a major change in the character, nature, organization, and competence of the arms acquisitions in that country. The Haganah was saved from a break with the official Zionist institutions. It established a secret, informal body of wealthy Jews who were willing to take the necessary risks to acquire the arms needed in establishing a Jewish army and a Jewish state, and which had tremendous influence on both the Jewish and non-Jewish public in the United States. In this way, the Haganah was able to garner the support of the official Zionist organizations as active partners in its legal actions, and as passive supporters of the illegal actions of arms acquisition after the war.

World War II ended without any meaningful arms acquisition activity in the United States, by either Etzel or the Haganah. At the same time, the war served to bring the plight of the Jews to the world and to create a profound feeling of guilt by the Jews of the United States, mixed with a desire to atone for their previous inaction. What the war period had contributed to the arms acquisition which took place after the war was the training of Jewish pilots and military men, the creation of an organizational basis for recruiting personnel, preparing the ground for secret work, primarily of the Haganah, and creating a readiness and spirit of sacrifice for the establishment of a Jewish state and a Jewish army in Palestine.

The Sonneborn Institute

According to most of the evidence in our possession, the idea of acquiring armaments machinery in the United States was that of the engineer Chaim Slavin.

Already at the end of 1944, Slavin reasoned that the end of the war would bring about a change in the military industrial system of the United

States. Many of the armaments manufacturers would be converting to the production of civilian needs, and most of the machinery used in producing arms would be sold off very inexpensively, as scrap metal. "I therefore sat down one night and wrote a letter to the supreme command of the Haganah, in which I described the fantastic possibilities opening up for us to buy surplus United States government equipment, so that we would finally be able to set up a real armaments industry.[42"]

Chaim Slavin

---

42 Yosef Evron, "Mechonot Yitzur MeiArzot HaBrit" (Manufacturing Machinery from the United States), HaTa'asiyah HaBithonit BeYisrael (The Defense Industry in Israel), Ministry of Defense Publications, Tel Aviv, 1980, pp. 77 ff. (Henceforth: The Defense Industry in Israel). So too: Interview of Uri Milstein with Chaim Slavin, Davar HaShavu'a, January 19, 1973. See also Dominique LaPierre and Larry Collins, Yerushalayim, Yerushalayim (O Jerusalem), Weidenfeld and Nicholson, Sifriyat Ma'ariv, Jerusalem, 1972 (Henceforth: O Jerusalem), pp. 55-56: When reading the newspaper that evening, Chaim Slavin noted a small item from Washington. In the next few months, seven hundred thousand new and almost new machines of the American armaments industry would be thrown out as scrap, said the item. Slavin wrote a letter to Ben-Gurion. To the Yishuv, he said, this was an unrepeatable opportunity. He begged that these machines be obtained and smuggled into Palestine in order to lay the foundations of a modern arms industry.

Slavin's proposal was brought to the attention of Ben-Gurion, but at the end of 1944 the heads of the Yishuv and the Haganah did not yet believe that this was practical, and Slavin remained unemployed and frustrated. The supreme command of the Haganah was in favor of setting up another manufacturing plant parallel to the existing one, but the implementation of the decision was faced with the vehement opposition of the existing manufacturing system[43].

When Ben-Gurion arrived in New York in June 1945, He stayed at Hotel 14, which was also known as "Kibbutz 14," as it served as the organizational headquarters of the Haganah personnel. He invited Meir Weisgal to his room, and this is what Weisgal reported about that meaning:

> I found Ben-Gurion sprawled on a large bed, like a pasha. The meeting, at which only the two of us were present, lasted about three hours. He told me at length what he wanted. The main thing was: Can you find 30 Jews who will follow me blindly, and who will do what I ask without asking questions? Afterwards, he told me his view regard the battle which was shaping up in Palestine after the war, the danger which the Yishuv would face, the need to obtain money, machinery, science, craftsmen, etc[44].

Weisgal acceded to Ben-Gurion's request and introduced him to Henry Montor, "who had been blessed with a brilliant talent to raise money and knew everyone worth knowing."[45] Montor gave Ben-Gurion a list

---

43 See: The Defense Industry in Israel, pp. 77-78.
44 See: Meir Weisgal, Ad Kan (Up to Here), Weidenfeld and Nicholson, Sifriyat Ma'ariv, Jerusalem, 1972, p. 180.
45 Ibid. p. 180.

of 17 "wealthy people, who could be trusted in their loyalty to the defense of the Yishuv.[46]"

Ben-Gurion met with his friend, the millionaire Rudolph G. Sonneborn, the Controller of a wealthy corporation which was involved in oil and in the chemical industry. During World War I Sonneborn had been a pilot in the air force of the United States Navy and in 1919 he had gone along with a request by a family friend, Louis D. Brandeis, to attend the peace conference in Versailles as the secretary of the American Zionist delegation. After the conference, Sonneborn had visited Palestine, and while sailing to it had become acquainted with David Ben-Gurion[47].

Now, 26 years after their first meeting, Ben-Gurion asked Sonneborn "to gather together in his home a number of people for a vital purpose.[48]"

After receiving his agreement, Ben-Gurion sent a telegram to each of the 17 wealthy men whose names had been given to him by Henry Montor, and asked them all to come to Sonneborn's home on July 1, 1945, at 9:30 a.m., for a vital matter. All 17 of them came at the appointed time. In addition to Sonneborn and Ben-Gurion, there were Henry Montor and Meir Weisgal, and on the Palestinian side, Eliezer Kaplan and Reuben Shiloah (Zaslani). The other participants were[49]:

Harold J. Goldenberg – Minneapolis
Julius Fligelman - Los Angeles

---

46 See: BaDerekh LeTzava UleMedinat Yisrael (On the Way to an Army and to the State of Israel), Article 37, April 1964.
47 See: The Trustees, pp. 18-19.
48 See: BaDerekh LeTzava UleMedinat Yisrael (On the Way to an Army and to the State of Israel), Article 37, April 1964.
49 Memo sent by Henry Montor to Ben-Gurion the next day (July 2, 1945), from the archive of the Institute for the Heritage of Ben-Gurion (henceforth: The Memo), (See Appendix B).

Shepard Broad - Miami

Philip Lown - Lewistown

Eli Cohen - Lyon

Ezra Shapiro – Cleveland

Albert Schiff – Columbus

Alex Lowenthtal - Pittsburgh

Charles J. Rosenbloom - Pittsburgh

William Sylk - Philadelphia

Sam Zachs - Toronto

Sam Chorr - New York

Jacques Torczyner - New York

Max Livingson - New Haven

Robert Travis - Atlanta

Adolf Hamburger - Baltimore

The meeting continued into the evening. Ben-Gurion lectured the assembled men about his conception:

We will in the near future be facing **all the Arab armies**, after the English leave the country. We will be able to stand up against them if we have the arms we need. In the destroyed and topsy-turvy world in Europe, we cannot be sure that we will obtain that which we had thought we would be able to obtain there.

The main point is that whatever arms the Haganah has obtained until now are only enough to face the local Arab bands, but not against **actual armies**, armed in most cases by Britain. It is essential for us to launch an arms industry soon - after the war [the United States was still fighting against Japan] we will have the possibility of purchasing, cheaply in this country, machines and tools needed for this... We will needs hundreds of thousands of dollars maybe even millions. Are you ready to supply the money needed for this[50]?

For hour after hour, they were bombarded with questions by those present. Ben-Gurion, Kaplan and Shilo'ach answered at length and in detail, and at the end of the meeting the 17 invitees promised to do whatever they could for the project. Five of them agreed to be the liaison with Ben-Gurion: Rudolph J. Sonneborn and Sam Chorr, of New York; Shepard Broad, of Miami; Harold G. Goldenerg of Minneapolis; and Julius Fligelman of Los Angeles[51].

That was how the "Sonneborn Institute," whose primarily involvement focused on secret arms acquisitions, was founded. Its mission was disguised as the supplying of equipment and medicines to hospitals. The Institute raised millions of dollars and helped in buying industrial machinery, weapons, ships and planes. It also helped in recruiting professional, scientific and military personnel.

Following the meeting in Sonneborn's house, Ben-Gurion wrote in his diary: "That was the best Zionist meeting I had in the United States.[52]" A few years later, Sonneborn wrote:

That unforgettable day we were asked to organize ourselves as the American branch of the Haganah underground. We were not given any hint as to what we would be required to do, when we would be required to do it, and who would be the one who would come to tell us what we were required to do. We were simply told to remain ready and to recruit Americans of similar viewpoints to ours. We were asked not to reveal the meeting[53].

---

50 See: BaDerekh LeTzava UleMedinat Yisrael (On the Way to an Army and to the State of Israel), Article 37, April 1964.
51 Memo
52 Ben-Gurion Diary, July 23, 1945, Vol. I, p. 516.
53 See: The Trustees, p. 23.

In October 1945 Chaim Slavin arrived in the United States, in order to arrange for the purchase of industrial machinery. In January 1946 Yaakov Dostrowski (Dori) arrived, and he brought Sonneborn new instructions. These instructions imposed defined tasks upon the Institute, which required it to reorganize as an executive committee[54].

The arrival of Dori in the United States signified the beginning of a new era, where the Haganah delegation embarked on secret and compartmentalized activities, which surpassed in range and method anything which had come before.

Organizational Development and Improvements in the Extent and Methods of Activity

Between January 1946 and April 1949, three individuals headed the Haganah delegation in the United States: a) Yaakov Dostrowski (Dori): January 1946 to June 1947 (18 months); b) Shlomo Rabinowitz (Shamir): June 1947 to February 1948 (9 months); Teddy Kolleck: February 1948 to April 1949 (14 months[55]). The three acted in coordinating the Palestinian armament requirements with those working at fulfilling these and the official Zionist organizations in the United States. The Sonneborn Institute worked with them, primarily in financing the costs, but also as an advisory body.

---

54 Ibid.pp. 73, 79.
55 Calculation regarding the Dori, Shamir and Kolleck eras, based on the following books: The Trustees, p. 73; Yerushalayim Ahat (One Jerusalem), Sifriyat Ma'ariv, Tel Aviv, 1979 pp. 79, 101; D. Ben-Gurion, Yoman HaMilhmah (Diary of the War) henceforth:Diary, edited by Gershon Rivlin and Dr. Elhanan Oren, Ministry of Defense Publ., Tel Aviv, 1982, Vol. 1, p. 204; Meir Pa'il, Mei"Haganah" LiTzeva Haganah (From the "Haganah" to the Defense Army), Zemora, Bitan, Modan, Tel Aviv, 1979, p. 92; Sefer Toledot HaHaganah (Book of the History of the Haganah) (henceforth: History of the Haganah), Vol. 3, p. 1235.

The armaments requirements were created as a result of a strange synthesis of lists of items which the High Command of the Haganah in Palestine prepared, and of the local initiative of activists in the armaments system in the United States itself, which involved taking advantage of opportunities which arose. The activity was secret and compartmentalized: the arms purchases were carried out by different bodies, which generally did not know of the others' existence. The head of the Haganah delegation thus had a most important position, because he was supposed to be the one who "knew everything." Along with his undercover work, the head of the delegation had to work in coordination with the political bodies which carried out their work openly and to steer his course based on the political - and military - developments in the Middle East and in the United States. Teddy Kolleck's description of his work can cast light on the extent of the functions of the delegation head:

> My work involved experiments in manufacturing weaponry, chemistry, and physics; discussions about buying ships; negotiating with factories and scrap yards; contacts with spies, gangsters, movie moguls, statesmen, bankers, professors, industrialists, and newspapermen; and there were plenty of illegal actions, from the most minor to ones of an international dimension. At every moment, the dream of the state was in danger. Slowly I found a way to deal with them. **It appeared to me that this position was too much for one person**, but it soon became clear that what was needed was a single coordinator to bring together the different kinds of experts with the work teams,

with advisors, with suppliers, and with financiers. One can say that I was a **traffic cop**....[56]

The extent of the work and the importance of the position as the head of the Haganah delegation in the United States was in inverse proportion to the short times the different heads served in that capacity. I will deal with this later on. First we will examine the organizational developments and the growth of the extent of activities throughout the times that each of the three served as head of the delegation.

The Yaakov Dostrowski (Dori) Period

When Dori was the head of the delegation, it was responsible for public relations, collecting funds, buying ships and "illegal immigration," acquiring arms, and primarily in acquiring machinery and equipment to manufacture weapons and armaments for the Jewish manufacturing industry. Slavin and those who worked with him were added to the delegation. Alongside Dori were Ze'ev Shind ("Dani"), who was involved in obtaining ships; Minna Rojozik (Ben-Zvi), who worked at collecting funds and ran the New York office; and Reuven Dafni, who was involved in collecting funds and weapons, and in preparing an infrastructure of helpers throughout the United States[57].

In order to acquire the machinery and to cover Slavin's activities, four fictitious corporations were established, a large warehouse in the New York suburbs was bought to store the purchases, special contacts

---

56 See: Yerushalayim Ahat (One Jerusalem), p. 80 (my emphasis).
57 See: Reuven Dafni, testimony at a seminar on "The Jews of America and the Establishment of the State of Israel," The Ben-Gurion University of the Negev, Beer Sheba, April 30, 1985. Similarly, Sefer Toledot HaHaganah (Book of the History of the Haganah) (henceforth: History of the Haganah), Vol. 3, p. 1235.

were initiated with those who loaded equipment in the New York harbor, young Jewish men of the youth clubs were enlisted to pack the goods, and special export licenses were prepared. Paralleling his activities in acquiring machinery, Slavin was involved in developing a machine gun along the lines of the Johnson machine gun. Most of this development took place in Canada.

In order to acquire the ships, twelve fictitious corporations were established, and their offices were rented in various places in the shipping area of Lower Manhattan. Connections were made with American Jews who owned ocean lines and with those who had had naval battle experience during World War II. The process of acquiring large ships for "illegal immigration" began, which brought about a major change in the number of immigrants to Palestine[58].

Reuven Dafni initiated connections with wealthy Jews in Miami Beach and Los Angeles, some legitimate businessmen and others members of the Mafia. Through one of the members of the Mafia, they managed to contact the president of Panama, who would later play a significant role in the arms acquisition activities in the United States[59].

Minna Rojozik, in addition to her activities in the financial realm, made contact with a Jewish ham radio operator named Reuben Gross, who was a lawyer by profession. Gross, a graduate of Harvard University and a military man in World War II, came to the offices of the Jewish Agency and volunteered to help. The Agency sent him to Minna Rojozik, and she supplied him with a B.C.

610 long-range transmitter which had been bought from war

---

[58] See: The Trustees, p. 75; similarly, Ze'ev (Vania) Hadari, Oniyot O Medinah (Ships or a State) (henceforth: Ships or a State), p. 34.

[59] See: Reuven Dafni, testimony, April 30, 1985.

surplus. In February 1946 Gross set up a communications center with the call letters W20XR, which was used by the New York delegation for ongoing communications with Tel Aviv. The messages were sent in encrypted form, three times a week, and they reported on the search for weapons, on Slavin's manufacturing facility, on the search for advisors, etc[60].

Dori made contact with a Jewish electronic engineer named Dan Fliderblum in order to buy a large amount of communications equipment, so as to set up a secret wireless network which would link the different settlements in Palestine[61].

During Dori's time as the delegation head, the operational areas, objectives, ties, and working methods of the Sonneborn Institute were established. The first deliberation of the Sonneborn Institute took place in the Astor Hotel in July 1946, exactly a year after the Ben-Gurion meeting in Sonneborn's home. At Sonneborn's suggestion, it was decided that the members of the Institute would meet each Thursday to hear updates, be given tasks, and for consultations. Sonneborn decided that the Institute representatives who took part in these meetings should organize within their own regions other groups to extend the influence of the Institute and to enlarge the number of supporters and contributors. On August 8, 1946, Sonneborn announced the enlargement of the supporters of the Institute by the addition of industrialists in the fields of the dairy industry, radio, sewing machines, advertising, naval supplies, and clothing. In a discussion held on October 17, 1946, it was decided to raise $100,000 a week, in order to have a kitty of a million dollars by the end of 1946. At the

---

60 See: The Trustees, pp. 91-97.
61 See: The Trustees, pp. 76-77.

beginning of 1947 the Institute's activities had spread throughout the United States, with dozens of different centers. In a meeting held on April 17, 1947 it became clear that based on an interim report of the Institute, in the three and a half months since the beginning of the year contributions had totaled $505,177.80.

The raucous actions of the "American League for Free Palestine," which represented Etzel and the Kook group, brought about the formation, at the beginning of 1947, of a parallel group by the Sonneborn Institute, which was named "Americans for the Haganah."

As the Institute expanded its reach and activities, it formalized a number of departments. An efficient financial department was created, led by Louis Booker, a very experienced stock trader, whose personal safe was used for the Haganah's treasury; as well as a public relations department headed by Harold Jaffar. The Institute staff opened a branch in New York in the Fisk Building, at 250 West 57th Street, corner of 8th Avenue, close to Columbus Circle.

In 1947, the Institute's activities extended to thousands of individuals, who were involved in it in various ways. The Institute's members organized home meetings which increased the awareness of the United States Jews as to what was happening in Palestine and in Europe. In addition to this, the Institute continued its secret and illegal work, and contributions to it were demanded beyond the contributions to other organizations and separate from them. Dostrowski acted in full coordination with Sonneborn. The increase in activities required the latter to appoint a deputy, who would be the link between the

Institute and the Haganah delegation head. This position, which played a dominant role in coordination between the Haganah and the "Institute," was filled by the industrialist Adolf Robison[62].

In the spring of 1947, by the time Dostrowski returned to Palestine, he could chalk up a string of achievements, the most important ones being the purchase of two Canadian Korvettes and the President Warfield cruise ship, which would later be known as the "Exodus"; the purchase of machinery; the making of important contacts; the achievement of the broad support of American Jewry, and the establishment of a wide-scale administrative apparatus. Dostrowski returned to Palestine on June 17, 1947, as Chief of Staff in accordance with Ben-Gurion's decision, where the aim was to change the strategic goals of the Haganah[63].

The Shlomo Rabinowitz (Shamir) Period

Rabinowitz arrived in the United States in December 1946, and worked in tandem with Dori until June 1947. In the second half of 1947, the activities of "Americans for the Haganah" intensified, as expressed in the publication of a magazine, the distribution of information leaflets, obtaining the support of various notables, and the organization of mass rallies. In a meeting of the Sonneborn Institute on October 25, 1947 at the Waldorf Astoria hotel, about a month before the UN vote on

---

62 Ibid.pp. 73-84.
63 A letter whose topic was "determinations," of June 16, 1957. In that letter, Galili was appointed as Chief of Staff and Ratner as military advisor by the Jewish Agency Executive. Arkhion Toledot HaHaganah (Archive of the History of the Haganah), File 73/107, in Mei"Haganah" LiTzeva Haganah (From the "Haganah" to the Defense Army), p. 92, p. 396 (Note 25).

the partition plan, Sonneborn announced: "We now have at least one member in every Jewish congregation in the United States. We now number about eighteen thousand members throughout the country."[64]

When Rabinowitz took over as the head of the Haganah delegation, he found himself swamped with proposals from the Sonneborn Institute and from the Jewish Agency offices in New York. All these initiatives required that each proposal be examined carefully. This required the expansion of both the number of fields in which the Institute should be involved and of the work within each field. The initiative of Al Schwimmer was without a doubt one of the most important and significant in terms of expanding the arms procurement activity.

Al Schwimmer, a Jewish flight engineer who had been employed by T.W.A. ever since 1942, came up with the idea of transporting Jewish refugees from Europe to Palestine by air. In August 1947 he discussed his idea with one of the Jewish Agency officials in New York, and a month later he was invited by Rabinowitz to prepare a detailed program which would include flight routes, the number of planes needed, and all the other needs for carrying out this plan. Schwimmer's plan was ready within two weeks, but only in November 1947 was he invited to Rabinowitz for the third time[65]. Rabinowitz introduced him to Yehudah Arazi (who was referred to as "Mr. Miller"), who was one of the central figures in the Haganah acquisitions system, and who generally worked independently while coordinating directly with Ben-Gurion and Eliezer Kaplan[66].

---

64 See: The Trustees, p. 103 (my emphasis).
65 See: Wings of Victory, pp. 107-108; Yaakov Erez, interview with Al Schwimmer, Ma'ariv, December 26, 1986.
66 See: Yerushalayim Ahat (One Jerusalem), p. 84.

The meeting between them led to the forming of the "Schwimmer Corporation Ltd." On December 12, 1947, Ben-Gurion received a message from Arazi that he had bought three Constellation and ten C-46 ("Commando") planes. So too did Arazi inform him that he was "depressed,"as "they had cut by two-thirds" that which had been promised to him[67].

Shlomo Shamir

---

67 See: Ben-Gurion, War Diary, Vol. 1, p. 41.

Arazi's budgetary problem and the chance of buying airplanes required Sonneborn to convene a special meeting of the Institute on December 11, 1947 to raise another five million dollars by the end of the year, in order to meet its "obligations." During 1947, the Institute had already raised more than two million dollars, and Sonneborn nevertheless wanted to obtain credit should they not have sufficient funds, or to have the Institute's members help by signing as partial guarantors, so that the Jewish Agency would be able to take out a five million dollar loan[68].

Al Schwimmer (on the right) with Leo Gardener and Leonard Dishek

---

68 See: The Trustees, pp. 116-117. Similarly, see: Ben-Gurion, War Diary, Vol. 1, p. 47. Ben-Gurion relates that Eliezer Kaplan, who was in the United States at the time (he had arrived in New York on November 30, 1947) in order to collect funds, made a fast trip to Jerusalem. "He gave an advance of 5 million dollars toward the United Appeal and wants to know how to divide the money." On Kaplan's trips to the United States, see: Ben-Gurion, War Diary, Vol. 1, p. 14. The purchase of arms required a large amount of cash to be raised in a very short time. See: Yerushalayim Ahat (One Jerusalem), pp. 91-93.

Another area which was enlarged, and for which a new framework was established, was Intelligence. Rabinowitz asked Nahum Bernstein, a successful lawyer in Manhattan, who had served as a lecturer in a secret OSS school during World War II, to open a secret school in the heart of New York, to train young Palestinian men in Intelligence work. The religious school of the National Council of Young Israel, on West 16th Street, was used by Bernstein to give a course in spying and served as a cover for the participants, who could appear to be night school students. In this course, the young men learned communications, encryption, sabotage, breaking and entering, hand-to-hand fighting, and how to wiretap. This "school" trained about fifty students, who were known as the "Shu-shu graduates," and were meant to engage in espionage. Some of them also helped in the arms acquisitions. The "school" also helped to encrypt the messages sent by Gross to Tel Aviv[69].

Another area of activity which became a major one was the collecting of arms. Many Jews who had served in the United States armed forces in World War II still had weapons or other military equipment in their possession. As the awareness of what the Haganah was doing increased, more and more people offered to donate these items to the Haganah. As these could hardly be sent by mail, the Haganah delegation had to set up branches and to appoint "roving ambassadors" to collect the arms and equipment. Americans, both Jewish and non-Jewish, were involved in this, including Harry Weinsaft, Sam Sterling, Brett Keating, Zimmel Roznik, and others[70].

---

69 See: The Trustees, pp. 88-95.
70 Ibid. pp. 97-101.

The Commitment

In December 1947 Arazi concluded two arms acquisition deals with a merchant named Leonard Weissman: 200 tons of explosives and an aircraft carrier. Nahum Bernstein, had also become the legal advisor to the Sonneborn Institute, cast doubts about the possibility of really acquiring an aircraft carrier. In spite of Bernstein's doubts, Arazi bought the ship for $125,000, and had it sailed to Norfolk for refurbishing, because by American law an aircraft carrier which was sold as war surplus had to have all military equipment removed, and this applied especially to the ability to launch and land planes on its deck[71].

Ben-Gurion assigned Rabinowitz to Jewish-American veterans who had had military experience in World War II, and who could help organize a modern army[72]. In working on this project, Rabinowitz reached Col. David ("Mickey") Marcus, Major Ben Dunkelman (the Queen's Regiment, Canada), General Ralph Smith, and a number of other officers. On December 30, 1947, Ben-Gurion received a message from Rabinowitz, in which the latter asked to return to Palestine[73].

On January 3, 1948 the arms acquisition project hit a major impediment, because of an error in loading at the New York dock in

---

71 Ibid. pp. 117-122, Ben-Gurion, War Diary, Vol. 1, p. 86.
72 See: Ben-Gurion, p. 684. Dori notes that "beyond the shortage in arms, there is a lack of the High Command. There are not enough commanders to direct battle plans and for staff work. This is something which requires experience and study. How does one overcome this? One needs a great outside expert to direct the members of the organization." See: Ben-Gurion, War Diary, Vol. 1, p.62. Also see: Ben-Gurion, War Diary, Vol. 1, pp. 86-87 ("Shlomo Shamir and Marcus traveled to San Francisco to see Smith"), and p. 191 ("There are no high-level officers in the country. We need brigadiers and generals"); similarly: Ben Dunkelman, Ne'emanut Kefulah (Dual Loyalty), Schocken, Tel Aviv, 1977, p. 100 ("They (Shamir and Marcus) came to inform me that the Haganah Command had decided to recruit military men with battle experience").
73 See: Diary, Vol. 1, p. 88.

Jersey City. As a result, 26 crates of TNT and 512 crates of industrial machinery[74] were seized and things unraveled, and more and more shipments were exposed.

The desire to hasten the arms acquisitions made Ben-Gurion decide in January 1948 that he needed to go to the United States once more[75]. The need to speed up the raising of money and of arms acquisition stemmed primarily from a serious crisis in the Haganah's finances and the plan to combine its finances with those of the Joint. On the other hand, there were but four months until May 15, when the British were to leave Palestine, and the Palestinian Jews had no air force, no navy, and no heavy artillery.

Because of the situation in Palestine, and because of the opposition of most of the members of the Executive to Ben-Gurion's leaving the country at that crucial juncture, Golda Meir went instead of him, on January 22, 1948[76], and on February 3, 1948 Rabinowitz returned to Palestine, accompanied by Col. Marcus[77].

Rabinowitz left the United States just as the crisis regarding arms acquisition was at its peak: arrests had been made, the smuggling from the New York harbor had been stopped, offices, warehouses, and dozens of operatives had been uncovered, and the FBI had turned up the heat. In spite of the criticism by Leonard Slater in his book, **The Trustees**, of Rabinowitz, claiming that the latter was of a suspicious nature and without imagination or initiative and did not know how to capitalize on the wave of commitment by many United States Jews on behalf of the Haganah and Palestine, one cannot deny that during the

---

74 See: The Trustees, pp. 11-15.
75 See: Diary, Vol. 1, p. 139.
76 Ibid.p. 168.
77 Ibid.p. 204.

Rabinowitz period the foundations for the acquisition of planes had been laid and the acquisition of ships had been expanded.

The Teddy Kolleck Era

Teddy Kolleck arrived in the United States in October 1947, and up to February 1948 he worked in tandem with Rabinowitz. The crisis in arms acquisition which had been caused on February 3, 1948 by one of the crates bursting open as it was being loaded onto the ship Executor, required a change in the methods used and of the cover story. There was a need to abolish a number of fictitious corporations, lest they be revealed for what they were. At the same time they had to open new offices and to establish new fictitious corporations. Nahum Bernstein, who was both involved in Intelligence and was a lawyer, helped them find new covers and to arrange for these corporations to be legally licensed. He guided his colleagues, many of them experienced lawyers, in setting up dummy corporations, subsidiary corporations, and legal entities which would take maximal advantage of the United States law. "Palestinians," he said, "are only interested in the final results. They do not know how to work under American conditions. They do not know how to achieve these things and what legal means they can employ." As a general rule he told them, as he had told Kolleck, "we need a broad organization to achieve all types of things, and a number of smaller organizations, which work undercover, to carry out special assignments"[78].

In accordance with the new policy, a total separation was made between "white goods," which could be dealt with openly and legally, and "black goods," which required secrecy and were illegal.

---

78 See: The Trustees, p. 58 (my emphasis).

At a meeting of the Institute on January 27, 1948 Sonneborn announced that the Institute's activities had now entered a new and decisive phase. "The four months which remain until the British leave Palestine require the Haganah to transform itself from a defense organization to an effective fighting force which is able to defend the nation," he said. "The Haganah needs wide-scale recruiting, both quantitatively and qualitatively, and the task of the Institute will be to help recruit volunteers from the United States and to equip the Jewish army, and not with money but with equipment."[79]

Teddy Kolleck, who had received lists from the Haganah in Palestine as to what was needed, distributed these lists among the members.

On January 27, 1948 a company named "Goods for Palestine" went into operation. It was run by Julius Zarko ("Rusty") and Isaac Imber and openly collected medical supplies, clothing, shoes, camping equipment, cars, building and fortification materials, office equipment, public address systems, gasoline, etc. At the same time, another organization, entitled "The Corporation for Land and Work in Palestine" was founded, which was ostensibly meant to recruit people to work on farms in Palestine, but in practice worked to recruit soldiers for the Jewish army as pilots, soldiers, wireless operators, airplane mechanics, radar operators, artillery men, officers, naval officers, etc. A delegation arrived from Palestine to launch an information campaign throughout the United States, which was run nationally by Major Wellesley Aaron. Offices were opened in Chicago, Boston, Philadelphia, Baltimore, Pittsburgh, Cleveland, Detroit, and Miami. Often, the two organizations shared the same facilities and

---

79 Ibid.pp. 158-159.

personnel. Lists were prepared of all the Jewish soldiers of the United States and Canada who had been discharged ever since the end of the war, and by means of letters and meetings they were called upon to volunteer. Harold Jaffar ran an orientation facility in Tel Aviv for all the volunteers from the English-speaking countries, and in this fashion 1500 volunteers were recruited from the United States and Canada[80].

Dealing with "black goods" required the establishment of corporations just to deal with these. "The Continental Corporation for Machinery and Metals," run by Phil Alper and Bob Keller, dealt with collecting and buying weapons, ammunition, and other types of military materièl. Up to January 1948 both had been involved in buying machinery for Slavin. Because of the discovery of the goods in New York Harbor on January 3, Phil Alper was arrested and four fictitious corporations were revealed. After he was freed under bail, they resumed what they had been doing but under a new cover and in a much larger scope[81].

"The Eastern Development Corporation," run by Sam Slavin and Moshe Heyman, dealt with developing armaments. The corporation employed in its "West Side Plant," or as it was known, "the Bird," a group of advanced students in the sciences and engineering, who devoted themselves primarily to developing a bazooka which the Haganah would use in the war[82].

The Wireless Communication Engineering Corporation, run by Danny Fliderblum, continued to buy communications equipment. Here too, the need to establish a new goal-specific corporation which

---

80 Ibid. pp. 160-166; 184-193.
81 Ibid. pp. 168.
82 Ibid.pp. 169-171.

would deal with communications equipment stemmed from the fact that when the Executor shipping case was exposed, communications equipment was found among the other goods.

David Bennett, one of Fliderblum's friends, was enlisted to run a subsidiary concern which dealt with radar equipment. Bennett also built a secret radar station next to Poughkeepsie, New York, which was used to train Palestinian young men[83].

The shipping of new materials obtained by the "Goods for Palestine" corporation throughout the United States required the formation of a shipping corporation. Harris Klein, a member of the Institute and a lawyer who specialized in truck shipping, set up a network of 150 truck shipping companies from coast to coast, which transported all the legal and "black" goods without charge. Klein arranged all the loading and unloading of cargoes by phone, keeping in constant contact with Rusty Zarko, who was in charge of routing. About three quarters of the owners of these shipping companies were Jews, but non-Jews, too, carried out this work faithfully. The shipping companies carried the goods to warehouses in Los Angeles, San Francisco, Denver, Chicago, New Orleans, and New York, and they remained there until they were loaded onto ships.

In New York, the Goods for Palestine Corporation had four warehouses for "white goods.[84]" As to the "black goods," another, secret warehouse was employed. Teddy Kolleck's assistant, Zvi Brenner, was in charge of these goods. An industrial building agent from Brooklyn, Morris Dolgin, obtained for Brenner a three story building which had previously been used as a preserves and meat packing plant. The

---

[83] Ibid.p. 172.
[84] Ibid.p. 163.

building was purchased in the name of Irving Strauss (Schwimmer's brother-in-law), and as a cover for what the building was really used for, Strauss opened up the Sherman Metropolitan Corporation. This company used the packaging and labels of the previous owner in order to disguise gunpowder as cans of preserves. The packing house served to house the goods which had been collected by Sam Sterling, Zimmel Reznik, Harry Weinsaft, and others. Pistols, machine guns and mortars were packed using the Alper-Shalit method into used industrial machinery[85].

In addition to the Sherman company, there were other storehouses for "black goods," such as scrapyards whose owners were part of the Institute, an open field in the Red Hook section of Brooklyn, and an empty quarry near Woodbury in Long Island (whose owner was Moshe Hyman[86]).

The "Executor Incident" brought about the annulment of contracts to transport goods by ship to Palestine. One of the owners of the American Export Lines said to Eli Shalit: "You should not be deluded by fantasies. Seven nations are fighting against the Jewish state. Do you think that you have any chance at all? We have to be realistic." Like other companies, the American Export Lines temporarily canceled all its sailings to Palestine. This development brought about the establishment of the American-Israeli Shipping Corporation by Eli Shalit and Raphael Recanati. This company leased Greek, Panamanian and even Lebanese ships to transport the goods. In order to transport the "black goods," Shalit hired Jules Chander and David Marsten, who

---

85 Ibid.pp. 172-174.
86 Reuven Dafni, Interview, Yad Vashem, Jerusalem, June 12, 1985.

specialized in packaging "black goods" under the guise of original shipments of famous companies such as Ford, General Motors, etc[87].

The Schwimmer Aviation Company was also under investigation by the FBI. In order to legitimate Schwimmer's activities before the authorities, there was the need to acquire two other airlines: Service Airways, which was owned by a Jew named Irving Schindler ("Swifty") and Lineas Aerease de Panama (in short LAPSA), the company which was meant to be the national airline of Panama[88].

At first, the deal was made with Schindler, which enabled them to buy three Constellation planes and to open a Panamanian airline. In accordance with the contract which Bernstein arranged, Schindler was defined as the president of the new Service Airways, Steve Schwartz was the vice-president, and Ray Sylk was the second vice president.

By contacting Martin P. Belfond, who was the owner of an independent airline named World Airlines, they clarified the possibility of buying LAPSA. On February 15, 1948 a contract was signed between LAPSA and Service Airways. The conditions of the contract permitted LAPSA not only to fly planes to Panama, but to also be permitted to "rent and lease out airplanes of any kind ... to maintain, operate, and repair factories and ports, buildings, hotels, garages, runways, airports ... to create, build, buy, sell, operate, rent out, rent, administer, repair, plan[89] .... The possibilities were limitless. In addition, the government of Panama was supposed to instruct its embassies and consulates overseas to request landing rights for LAPSA planes throughout the world.

---

87 See: The Trustees, pp. 181-183.
88 See: Wings of Victory, p. 109.
89 See: The Trustees, p. 198.

The contract with LAPSA made it possible for the air activity to expand markedly. In order to achieve greater independence in running the company, it was necessary to shift its operating center from the United States to Panama. The Burbank airport became the overhauling center and more than two hundred mechanics were employed there. The idea was that after a plane was overhauled it would then be sent to Malul for the final fittings and inspections. After a number of planes were ready in Malul, they would all fly down to Panama.

Pilots' Course in Bakersfield: from left to right: Paltiel Makleff, David Dankner, Sarah Guberman (Makleff), Zahara Levitov; Meir Hofshi

The need to buy arms legally required various contacts in order to find a country which would be willing to buy arms for the Haganah and with its money. Not only did the British mandate forbid the members of the Yishuv from owning arms, but it did everything possible to prevent the Yishuv from buying arms legally. That was also what other nations did. One of the Zionist leaders in the United States arranged a contact with General Somoza, the Nicaraguan ruler. Teddy Kolleck flew to Managua, the capital of Nicaragua, and when he arrived there he obtained two diplomatic Nicaraguan passports: one for Yehudah Arazi and one for himself. In addition to the passports, Kolleck received letters authorizing the purchase of machinery and weapons in the amount of three million dollars, which were meant for the Nicaraguan ambassador in Paris and its general consul in Zurich. These letters enabled him to legally purchase machinery and arms in France and in Switzerland[90].

During the time Kolleck served in this position, the ties with Mexico were also expanded. Hank Greenspun, who was responsible for buying weaponry and in collecting it on the West Coast and in Hawaii, had the weaponry loaded onto ships in California, which was then sent via Mexico, Hawaii, and the Philippines. The contacts with Mexico served as a useful cover for transporting "black goods" from the West Coast, ostensibly to Mexico. In addition, the contacts with Mexico enabled the Haganah to purchase weapons and cannon from the Mexican army[91].

Teddy Kolleck's contacts with Sam Rudnick, one of the wealthiest men in the United States, brought about the establishment of a flying school for the Haganah in Bakersfield, California. Eleanor Rudnik, who was herself a pilot and active in the "Americans for Haganah," supplied all the needs of the school, whereas the Bakersfield Jews

---

90 See: Yerushalayim Ahat (One Jerusalem), pp. 82-83.
91 Ibid.p. 81. Similarly, Eliyahu Sakharov, Interview, March 11, 1985.

supplied all the personal needs of the students, such as pocket money, laundry, cigarettes, meals, etc. This school was active from March through June 1948, and trained 13 pilots who were able to fly in the War of Independence. Four of them fell in that war[92]. One of the most famous of its graduates was Oded Abarbanel, a distinguished El Al pilot.

Danny Shind's actions to purchase ships were also expanded. Now there was the need not only to buy ships to bring in "illegal immigrants," but also ships for the Jewish navy. Throughout 1947, when Shind was forced to stay in Genoa because of kidney stones, David Nameri was sent to the United States and dealt with purchasing war surplus frigates, small boats, and spare parts[93].

Three American Jews were the main individuals who helped in this task: Morris Ginsberg, Joe Buxenbaum, and Paul Schulman. On March 3, 1948, Ben-Gurion send a telegram to Moshe Sharett asking him to send to Palestine "two or three Jewish naval personnel," and even asked: "Can Paul Schulman come"[94]? Schulman accordingly came to the country in May. In November 1948 Ben-Gurion awarded Schulman the rank of major general and appointed him the first commander of the first commander of the Navy

---

[92] See: Wings of Victory, pp. 101-104, 337 - the names of the graduates of the course.
[93] David Nameri, testimony, Document 4396 in the History of the Haganah Archive.
[94] Telegram to Ben-Gurion from Shertok, March 3, 1948, History of the Haganah Archive, Ben-Gurion File, No. 17, Diary, Vol. 1, p. 276 (March 3, 1948.)

Major General Nahman (Paul) Schulman, first commander of the Navy

The Declaration of Independence on May 14, 1948 did not bring about a substantive change in arms acquisition. Now, though, rather than representing the Haganah, Kolleck represented the Ministry of Defense of the State of Israel. The recognition de facto which the United States granted the provisional government of the State of Israel did not change United States policy. Thus the activities continued to be secret.

The intensification of the War of Independence, together with the organizational expansion of the arms acquisition entities in the United States and the increased identification of American Jews with the young Jewish state which was struggling for its life, brought about a sizable growth, both qualitatively and quantitatively, in the arms acquisition activity. Teddy Kolleck's period was marked by a significant expansion in arms acquisition, and his contribution to Israel's great victory in the War of Independence was most significant.

The Organizational Preparations of the Etzel for Arms Acquisition in the United States

The actions of the Hebrew Committee for National Liberation were generally in accordance with the ideological premises of Etzel, but the fact that on occasion these were not coordinated was a cause of friction. Furthermore, up to the spring of 1946 the Committee did not supply any direct financial aid to Etzel, in spite of its fund-raising campaign[95].

Etzel's decision to engage in an open struggle with the British brought about a second front against the British in Europe. To coordinate this, Etzel sent a delegation to Italy in January 1946, whose primary purpose was to coordinate all Etzel activities in the diaspora. In addition, the delegation was entrusted with other objectives, involving the recruiting of soldiers among the surviving European Jews and training them in how to sabotage British installations throughout the world, and to recruit financial, military and political support for Etzel's activities[96].

Only in April 1947 did the Etzel command in the diaspora establish a central financial department, headed by Dr. Y. Lipschitz (Shiloni). It was the task of this department to solicit funds and to supervise the solicitation campaigns run on behalf of Etzel in the United States and other countries. It was decided that 25% of the funds gathered in the diaspora would be used for local needs. In the United States, campaigns were launched for Etzel by the Hebrew Committee for

---

95 See: HaHazit HaSheniyah (The Second Front), p. 49 (note 54), p. 34.
96 Ibid. p. 9.

National Liberation and by HaTzohar. The friction and competition between the two caused the command to established a separate branch to take care of all of the funds in the United States, which was called the Palestine Emergency Fund. The solicitations for what Etzel termed "the Steel Fund," reached their peak at the end of 1947. They were run primarily by an organization called The American League for a Free Palestine. The author Ben Hecht, who was one of the main activists in the League, composed Etzel's advertisements, which frequently compared the British to the Nazis and what was happening in Palestine to a new Holocaust. The League organized mass demonstrations in which musicians, dancers, singers and other notables appeared. Thus, for example, it organized such a pageant in New York to collect funds under the title of "We Will Never Die." Hecht himself wrote the script and Billy Rose produced the pageant. Forty-thousand people came to see the event, which raised more than a million dollars during the period in which it was shown throughout the country[97].

The problem of fund-raising and the transfer of the money to Palestine was a constant and sensitive topic between the commanders in Palestine and the delegation in the diaspora. The United States was the largest source of funds for Etzel, and ongoing friction between the League and HaTzohar forced the command in Palestine to send Shmuel Katz to make peace between the two. In reality, Etzel had no way of checking how the money collected in the United States was divided up. The League's funds were all kept in New York by H. Selden and Y. Ben-Ami and were sometimes divided up against the wishes of the Command. The same was the fate of HaTzohar's funds[98].

---

97 See: The Trustees, p. 82.
98 See: HaHazit HaSheniyah (The Second Front), pp. 142-143.

Begin's appeal on February 1, 1948 to the Etzel supporters to help finance the preparations for repulsing the invaders and to expand the borders of the partition was met enthusiastically by the commanders of Etzel and its supporters. At this stage, all the campaigns in the United States were run by Dr. Lipschitz and S. Merlin, and they were aided by Betar graduates and the Revisionist Party. The money collected was sent to a Swiss bank, and from there it was smuggled to Palestine or was used to finance the necessary preparations. The Steel Fund was run openly and with the knowledge of the local authorities. The Jewish Agency representatives demanded that the Fund be abolished, claiming that Etzel was in the midst of negotiations about joining the Haganah, or that in any event it was about to be disbanded. In April 1948 the perpetual shortage of funds forced the Command to approach Rabbi Dr. Abba Hillel Silver formally and to request a one-time grant of half a million dollars from the Zionist Emergency Committee in the United States. Despite his sympathy for Etzel, Silver refused to intervene, lest he remain in the minority and his prestige in the committee would be affected[99]. It is possible that his refusal came from the very fact that he was aware of and appreciated the contacts taking place in Palestine between the Haganah and Etzel regarding the disbanding of Etzel after the Proclamation of the State.

On June 1, 1948, Menahem Begin signed, on behalf of Etzel, an agreement with the Provisional Government, as represented by Yisrael Galili. Under this agreement, the members of Etzel would join the Israel Defense Forces within a framework of battalions and would swear an oath of loyalty; their weapons and military equipment would be transferred to the Supreme Command of the IDF; Etzel and its command would cease to exist and act in the State of Israel and within

---

99 Ibid.p. 145.

the areas under the control of the Israeli Government. It was agreed that a temporary command of Etzel, which would act for no more than a month, would handle the enlistment of Etzel battalions into the IDF. Etzel also undertook to cease its arms acquisition activities abroad and to hand over the contacts its representatives had with arms sources to the representatives of the Provisional Government[100]. According to Chaim Landau (Avraham), Etzel's reaction regarding the future of the movement outside Israel was that "in the area controlled by a Hebrew government we will not maintain an armed underground, but we have not made any declarations regarding the other 'territories.' Of course we will continue to exist there, as, for example, in Jerusalem and outside Israel.[101]"At the same time, on September 2, 1948 the Etzel members in the United States received instructions from the Command in Jerusalem and from the diaspora department to cease their arms acquisition[102]. The disbanding of Etzel in Jerusalem in September 1948 affected all its emissaries abroad. They were all now eligible for the draft in accordance with Israeli law, and they could become deserters, who would be punished when they returned to Israel. When the Command received word that in order to stay abroad its representatives abroad would have to apply for an exemption from enlistment, all its representatives were all informed of this by the Command, which then left the decision to them as to whether to return and enlist or to remain in the diaspora[103].

The Etzel activity in the United States between 1945 and 1948 focused primarily on collecting money, along with various spectacular actions to gain public support. At the same time, Etzel was involved in a very

---

100 See: Ben-Gurion, Vol. 2, "On the Verge of Civil War," p. 777.
101 See: HaHazit HaSheniyah (The Second Front), p. 139.
102 Ibid. p. 254.
103 Ibid. pp. 241-242, 260.

small number of clandestine actions. Thus, for example, Avraham Stavski ("Abrasha") opened a shipping line named the Three Star Line, whose offices were on Madison Avenue in Manhattan, New York. The declared aims of the company were commercial, whereas its members tracked various ocean-going vessels as they sought to obtain ones for "illegal immigration." The expert in this was Jack Bruin[104]. In 1946 the Hebrew Committee for National Liberation helped in obtaining two "Illegal immigration" ships in Italy, the Divina Providenzia (which became the "David Raziel") and the Waga. The attempt to sail them to Palestine failed in both cases: the first went up in flames and the second disappeared[105]. In 1947 the Committee helped them to buy two other ships in the United States: the Ben Hecht for $170,000 and the Altalena for $250,000[106]. That was the end of the purchases by Etzel of ships in the United States.

The "Ben Hecht"

---

104 See: Shlomo Nekadimon, Altalena, Idanim, Jerusalem, 1978, pp. 12-13.
105 See: HaHazit HaSheniyah (The Second Front), pp. 61-63, 98.
106 Ibid.p. 145.

In 1947 the Etzel Command planned to fly "illegal immigrants" to Palestine. In France, they conducted negotiations to buy Lodestar planes and in the United States they set up a "Club for Demobbed Pilots," whose aim was to prepare pilots for this operation. There were about fifty pilots in the Club, all of whom had combat experience from World War II, who trained in leased planes. The head of the Club was an Etzel member named Spektor, who was a friend of Peter Bergson[107].

On February 25, 1948, Hyman Shamir arrived in the United States as an emissary of the Haganah. He came to help in the acquisition of planes and in recruiting air crews[108].

He met with Spektor and his men in the Wellington Hotel in New York, in order to persuade them to join Al Schwimmer's group. At the meeting, attended by Hank Greenspun and Al Schwimmer, Spektor laid down tough conditions: a) the Etzel pilots would be a separate unit and would wear Betar uniforms; b) these pilots would not be considered part of the Haganah, even though they would live with its men; the pilots would be under the Etzel Command, and every order they received would require the approval of both Etzel and the Haganah. The meeting ended in a failure, in spite of the appeal by Hyman Shamir to transcend personal considerations in order to set up an air force. In spite of this, a few days later thirty pilots who were members of the Club joined Schwimmer's group, and some of them were among the most distinguished air force pilots in its first era (Ray Kurtz, Y. Reisen)[109].

---

107 See: Wings of Victory, p. 105.
108 See: Tzvi Dresnin, Hyman, HaIsh VeHaTekufah (Hyman, the Man and the Era), Zemora, Bitan, Modan, Tel Aviv, 1980, p. 53.
109 See: Wings of Victory, pp. 105-106.

Other clandestine work involved collecting arms, ammunition, and clothing. For this, a goods warehouse was bought in New York. A. Horowitz organized the shipment of packages from the United States to Palestine. In the period between February 6, and March 15, 1948, 43 packages of food arrived in Tel Aviv, each of which contained two revolvers and 200 bullets. Three packages contained the parts of a radio transmitter, and a number of packages contained medical supplies. The Etzel warehouse in New York held over two tons of explosives, but they could not find a way to send them to Palestine[110].

In comparison with what the Haganah had set up in the United States in order to arrange for underground arms acquisition, that of Etzel in that country was very limited. Internal disputes, poor communications with the "Command for the diaspora" and with the commanders in Palestine, a break with the official Zionist institutions, friction with the Haganah and flamboyant actions, prevented Etzel from setting up a large-scale and efficient underground arms acquisition system in the United States. In spite of this, there is no doubt that the work of the Committee influenced public opinion in the United States and drew Jews closer to the Zionist cause.

---

110 See: HaHazit HaSheniyah (The Second Front), pp. 197-198.

The license by the Panamanian government to sail the Altalena as a cargo vessel

Chapter 3:

Arms Acquisition and its Contribution to the War of Independence

Manufacturing Machinery

The arrival of Slavin in the United States in October 1945 marked the beginning of the process of acquiring manufacturing machinery. In spite of his talent as an engineer, and in spite of his untiring efforts to perform every task needed to meet his goals, Slavin was limited greatly by the fact that he was not fluent in English and was unfamiliar with the laws involved, with American practices, and with the opportunities the country offered. The person who helped Slavin to initiate contacts with experts and to buy machinery was Harry Levin. Levin was a devoted Zionist, a millionaire with a plastics factory in Leominster, Massachusetts, and in World War II was involved in arms manufacture as one of the owners of the New York Safe and Lock Company, which manufactured parts for the Swedish Orlikon cannon under a special license[111].

---

111 See: The Trustees, p. 33.

"Looking back," said Slavin, "I cannot even imagine what I would have done without him. How would I have overcome the obstacles in a foreign land, whose language I did not even speak, when I first came there? For me, he was far more than an acquaintance. He was a brother and friend who stood by my side, without fear, when I was an emissary of the Haganah: he never turned me away empty-handed; he was never too busy to give me of his time. He spoke for me, and his home was always open to me.[112]"

A machine to produce bullet casings bought by Slavin in the US

---

112 See: The Defense Industry in Israel, p. 78.

Saadiah Gelb, who was active in the Jewish Agency, introduced Slavin to a young engineer named Phillip Alper. In addition to Alper, Slavin was helped by a young Palestinian who was a member of the Haganah, who had spent considerable time in England and in the United States - Eli Shalit. While Slavin and Alper dealt primarily with searching for manufacturing equipment and assessing its technical value, Eli Shalit was responsible for packing and shipping whatever they had found, and for arranging export licenses. In order to give the shipments a patina of legitimacy, four fictitious companies were formed: the Manufacturing and Reconditioning Corporation; the Workers Trading Corporation; the Attic Trading Corporation; and the New England Plastic and Innovation Corporation[113]. The transport was carried out by the Hoffman Corporation, and the goods were packed in a warehouse at 4366 Park Avenue[114].

The search for manufacturing machinery was carried out both by open advertising and letters and through the W.A.A., which dealt with war surplus. The machines were sold as scrap at low cost, by tender or by auction. As there was great demand, there was the need to have a system of contacts which would guarantee that Slavin would be able to buy what he needed, and that no one else would outbid him. The machines were packed as textile machinery, agricultural machinery, etc. The work required dismantling the machines into small parts and documenting each so that they could be reassembled in Palestine. Slavin and his colleagues were helped in the packing by youths of the HaBonim and HeHalutz youth movements[115].

---

113 See: The Trustees, pp. 141-2; similarly: The Defense Industry in Israel, p. 79.
114 See: The Trustees, p. 40.
115 Sa'adiah Gelb - interview, Rehovot, May 22, 1985.

Eliahu Sakharov was responsible for taking care of the machines once they arrived in the country, and also helped in obtaining import licenses from Solel Boneh and from a number of private industrialists (legally, import licenses had to have the consent of the mandatory regime). According to Sakharov:

> Until then, there was no precedent in the history of the Haganah for shipments of that size and quantity. There were shipments which exceeded 200 tons in weight and which consisted of about 100 crates of machines, equipment, tools for manufacturing arms, and arms parts made in the United States or Canada. Some occupied an entire wharf and drew the attention of all the port's workers, as shipments of this magnitude had been very unusual in the port's history[116].

Machines to join bullets to casings, bought by Slavin in the US

---

116 Eliyahu Sakharov - testimony, in the Archives of the History of the Haganah, Document No 1202.

In the autumn of 1969, Rudolf Sonneborn estimated that no less than 250,000$ of the Institute's funds had reached the Swiss accounts of British officials in order to play dumb when Slavin's shipments arrived in Palestine[117].

Slavin and Alper prepared an informative catalog of everything which might be useful and which was for sale in the United States. With the aid of this catalog, they embarked on a shopping expedition. Their first purchase was from the Remington factory and included machines to manufacture bullets (some of these machines are still in use today!). The machines were bought by weight - seventy dollars per ton. Afterwards, they made a deal with Colt Arms, where they bought machines to produce light arms. Later, they bought machines to manufacture mortars, hand grenades, bullets, explosives, and even cannon barrels[118]. Up to the end of Slavin's assignment in the United States (December 1946) thirteen shipments of machine parts were shipped to Palestine, which included about 800 crates, about 95% of the equipment needed to start a bullets and explosives industry. Along with the purchase of the machinery, they also acquired vital information from Ignatz Gragirov, a Jewish engineer of Russian extraction, who, according to Slavin, passed him important information regarding the manufacture of explosives, as "a gift to the Jewish people". Another achievement in this realm was the acquisition of the "Olsen Patent" for manufacturing gunpowder for light arms[119].

Throughout his stay in the United States, Slavin made great efforts to acquire information on how to manufacture submachine guns. For

---

[117] Dominique LaPierre and Larry Collins, Oh, Jerusalem!, p. 57, note at the bottom of the page.
[118] Interview of Uri Milstein with Chaim Slavin, Devar Hashavu'a, January 19, 1973.
[119] See: The Defense Industry in Israel, p. 80; The Trustees, pp. 39, 43-47.

this purpose, he was able to meet a Swedish engineer named Carl Akadal, who had been one of those who had designed the Johnson submachine gun used by the US marines in World War II. The manufacturing was supposed to take place in Canada, and for that purpose a large workshop was set up in a car parts factory in Toronto. After six prototypes had been manufactured, they were discovered on February 24, 1947 when they were being taken across the border from Canada to the United States. A number of those involved were arrested[120].

In spite of this, five thousand manufacturing machines were sent to Palestine, along with various blueprints regarding the manufacture of a submachine gun, and at the beginning of 1948 they began to be produced in Palestine (under the name of Dror[121]).

The acquisition of the machines enabled the Haganah to set up twelve factories, which manufactured weapons and ammunition throughout the War of Independence. From October 1, 1947 until the second cease-fire in July, 1948 Slavin's companies manufactured about 16,000 Sten submachine guns, more than 150,000 Mills grenades, 210,000 3 inch mortars, more than 130,000 mortar shells, 4 million 9 mm. bullets, and many other items. The value of all of these was about 300,000 Palestinian Pounds, and their importance was immense[122]. An inventory of arms owned by the Haganah in September 1947 showed

---

120 See: The Trustees, pp. 59-65.
121 The Defense Industry in Israel, p. 80.
122 Y. Avidar, BaDerekh LeTzaHaL (On the Way to the IDF), Ma'arakhot, Third Edition, 1977, pp. 275, 276, 299. Similarly: Interview of Uri Milstein with Chaim Slavin, Devar Hashavu'a, January 19, 1973; Mei"Haganah" LiTzeva Haganah (From the "Haganah" to the Defense Army), p. 280.

2,666 submachine guns and 92 3 inch mortars[123]. The data regarding these two items shows us a growth of 600 percent in the number of submachine guns and more than 200 percent in the number of mortars, thanks to the production by the Slavin factories.

The Dror submachine gun

The acquisition of these machines in the United States is an example of the type of work the purchasing agents were involved in. Those involved defined their objectives, determined their priorities, and acted in accordance with whatever the conditions in the United States enabled them to act. These actions are proof that in the era after World War II it was possible to send out from the United States large machines weighing hundreds of tons. Why, therefore, did they not purchase other weapons at that time?

---

123 The inventory of arms as of September 1947, according to the Archive of the History of the Haganah, Ben-Gurion File No. 17, regarding the problems of defense before the establishment of the State, in which there appears a report of the inventory of arms as of September 15, 1947. From Mei"Haganah" LiTzeva Haganah, p. 280.

The Airplanes

On October 3, 1947 Ben-Gurion wrote in his diary:

> I gave instructions to America to buy airplanes and to recruit pilots, with the aim that some of them should come to [Palestine] immediately. The rest should be ready to come; [they should] recruit those who had been soldiers so that they would be ready to come. To find a top-rate expert with experience to come to the country[124].

In November 1947, Arazi purchased for the Schwimmer Company three Constellation planes at $15,000 each, and ten P-46 ("Commando") planes at $5,000 each[125]. Between January 1947 and January 1948 the planes were kept together in Burbank for maintenance. There was a need to remove the planes from the United States for a number of reasons: the intensified fighting in Palestine, the surveillance and harassment of the FBI, the new American law which was to go into effect on April 15, 1948, which would require a special authorization of the Armaments Supervision Committee for the export of heavy civilian and all military planes of any kind, and the embargo which the American government had imposed on the supplying of arms to the Middle East.

In December 1947 and January 1948 Ehud Avriel and Dr. Felix Doron initiated contacts with arms manufacturers in Czechoslovakia. The negotiations were concluded on January 14, 1948, with the first arms acquisition contract with Czechoslovakia, which included 4,500

---

124 See: Ben-Gurion Diary, October 3, 1947, in Ben-Gurion, Vol. 2, p. 660, 1072 (note 62).
125 See: Yoman HaMilhmah (Diary of the War) henceforth: Diary, Vol. 1, p. 412; The Trustees, pp. 195-201.

rifles, 200 submachine guns, and 5 million bullets. Officially, the contract was signed between Czechoslovakia and Ethiopia, and there is no doubt that this agreement was influenced by the positive attitude toward it by the Soviet Union[126].

Now, another reason arose for moving the planes from the United States: the Constellation and Commando planes, as they were transport planes, could ensure that the Czech contract could be consummated in the most speedy and efficient way if these planes were available[127].

A P-46 ("Commando") plane

---

126 See: Ben-Gurion, Vol. 2, p. 671 Similarly, Yoman HaMilhmah (Diary of the War), Vol. 1, pp. 45, 58-59, 110-111; Sefer Toledot HaHaganah (Book of the History of the Haganah) (henceforth: History of the Haganah), Vol. 3, p. 1526. Similarly, Shimon Peres, Kela David (David's Sling), Weidenfeld and Nicholson, Jerusalem, 1970, p. 20: "The decision to sell arms to Israel was that of the entire [Czech] Government, and possibly with the silent approval of Moscow. Nevertheless, the then-Secretary of the Communist Party in Czechoslovakia, Slanski, was accused of a 'Jewish-Zionist Plot' which he had allegedly 'cooked up' with Ehud Avriel, and he and a number of his assistants were 'sentenced' and executed" (my emphasis).

127 See: Colonel Binyamin Kagan, Heim Himri'i BeAlata (They Flew in the Darkness), Davar, Tel Aviv (henceforth: They Flew in the Darkness), p. 48.

The First Flight

At the end of February 1948, a single Commando plane was flown from Burbank to Melville, and after it was readied to fly across the ocean it left for Teterboro on March 6, for a Customs inspection. The Customs inspection was passed without any problem and the plane flew on to Italy. On March 9, the plane landed in Castiglione de Lago. The arrival of the plane in Italy enabled the Haganah to carry out its first arms purchase from the Czechs, but after intensive deliberation it was decided to refrain from doing so until all the planes had been removed from the United States, so as not to endanger their removal from that country. The plane remained in Italy, and after its crew decided that the earthen runway in Castiglione de Lago would not do, it was moved to the Foggia airport. The flight crew, which included Leo Gardener, Arnold Ilwit, Robert Fine, Sam Pomerantz, Ernest Stahlich (a non-Jew), and Irwin Schindler, continued to train, and even went to search for a ship named the Lino, which was carrying weaponry from Czechoslovakia to Syria. After Arnold Ilwit was able to fly the plane, Leo Gardener returned to New York[128].

A Constellation

---

128 See: Kanfei Nitzahon (Wings of Victory) (henceforth: Wings of Victory), pp. 117-118.

The first Constellation, which was flown by Sam Lewis, left New York on March 13, 1948, and landed in the Tocumen airport in Panama. There was a welcoming committee awaiting it, of senior civil servants, who gave fiery speeches about turning over of a new leaf in the economic life of Panama. The plane only arrived in Europe on June 25, 1948, and was used to transport the second arms purchase from Czechoslovakia and for different tasks in Palestine itself, until it was damaged in one of its landings in Czechoslovakia. This plane was grounded for a long time, until it was returned to the United States for repairs. From there it again returned to Israel, but that was already after the War of Independence, and it was used by the El Al airline.

After the first two planes had been removed from the United States, the Schwimmer company still had two Constellations and nine Commandos. The United States government managed to hold back the two Constellations, and they did not take part in the War of Independence. They were only allowed out of the United States after the cease-fire, and joined the El Al fleet[129].

The Second Flight

April 9 was set as the date for four Commandos to fly to Panama. The head of this flight was to be Hal Ohrbach. However, the flight was stopped by a government official, who claimed that "we do not authorize the departure of the planes." By the intervention of the lawyer of the Service Airlines, Nachum Bernstein, the planes left on April 10. During the flight, Ohrbach's plane was forced to land in

---

[129] Ibid.pp. 117-119.

Florida because of mechanical trouble, but it was repaired, the plane refueled, and continued to Tocumen. All four planes arrived safely in Panama[130].

The Third Flight

Permission to fly the last five Commandos was received on April 14, 1948. The planes flew from Los Angeles, heavily laden, and landed in Mexico City for rest and refueling. After they flew out of Mexico City, one of the planes exploded, and its crew, the pilot William Gershon and the mechanic Glen King, were killed. The other four planes landed safely in Tocumen. After the plane had exploded near Mexico City, the pilots raised a storm, claiming that the load they were carrying was far too heavy, that this was criminal, that there was disorder in the company, that the administration was faulty, that there were technical problems, etc. Hyman Shamir and Al Schwimmer arrived in Tocumen to calm things down and to give answers. Schwimmer said decisively: "We are doing the best we can. If you want a cushy job in an airline, it would be advisable for you to leave here.[131]" At this stage there were nine planes in Tocumen: one Constellation and eight Commandos. As noted, two Constellations still remained in the United States. In Tocumen, all types of rumors started flying about what the LAPSA company was up to, and governmental guards were posted around the planes. The depressed atmosphere hastened their desire to take off already and to fly across the sea[132].

---

130 Ibid.pp. 119-120; The Trustees, pp. 221-224.
131 See: The Trustees, p. 238.
132 Wings of Victory, p. 121.

The Fourth Flight

On April 23, 1948, a second arms deal was signed with Czechoslovakia, under which Israel bought 24,500 rifles, more than 5,000 light submachine guns (MG 34), 200 Beza machine guns, 54 million bullets, and 25 German Messerschmidt planes, along with their equipment and weaponry[133].

To send the Messerschmidts by sea would have taken four months. Therefore, it was decided to ship them by air inside the Commandos which were in Panama. However, they needed to find another European airport for an interim stop. Hyman Shamir and Dan Agronski conducted negotiations in Sicily, as a result of which they arranged for the use of the airport of Catania. Hyman Shamir presented himself as a representative of LAPSA, whereas Dani Agronski appeared as a representative of Services Airways[134]. After the two had received the required authorizations, they informed Al Schwimmer of this.

On May 8, 1948 a flight of five Commandos flew out of Tocumen via Brazil, Dakar, and Casablanca, and on May 15 the first two Commando planes arrived in Catania. The others were delayed along the way because of technical problems.

On May 16 the two Commando planes left Catania for Ekron, together with Hyman Shamir. On May 17, the two left for Zatec, in Czechoslovakia, in order to bring the Messerschmidt 109s. A few days later, the other Commando planes, which had been delayed along the way, arrived, and they, too, were involved in shipping materièl from Czechoslovakia to Israel. With the arrival of the last planes, the

---

133 See: Sefer Toledot HaHaganah (Book of the History of the Haganah), Vol. 3, p. 1526; Bar-Zohar, Ben-Gurion, Vol. 2, p. 671
134 See: Wings of Victory, p. 115

fourth flight came to an end. The project of moving materièl from Czechoslovakia to Israel was termed the Balak Operation[135] or the "Air Bridge."

The Fifth Flight

During May 1948 Teddy Kolleck continued in his position and was instructedto buy more airplanes[136]. Al Schwimmer looked for long-range heavy bombers.

On May 26, the Provisional Government issued Order No. 4, which dealt with the establishment of the IDF. The Haganah became the Israel Defense Forces and the Air Service became the Air Force[137]. The need for heavy bombers increased due to what was happening in the field in May 1948: on May 14, Gush Etzion fell, Arab armies invaded on May 15, and the Old City of Jerusalem fell on May 28[138].

Schwimmer's search led him to four B-17 Flying Fortresses and four A-20 Havocs. It was agreed that the price of each Flying Fortress would be $15,000 and each A-20 would cost $6,000. (For the purposes of comparison, for each Messerschmidt which they bought in Czechoslovakia they paid $190,000[139]).

In order to take the planes out of the United States, they had to find new crews and professionals who could renovate the planes. Leo

---

135 Ibid.pp. 122-123. Similarly, Ze'ev Schiff and Eitan Haber, Leksikon le-Bitahon Yisrael (Lexicon of Israel's Defense), Zemora, Bitan, Modan, Davar Edition, Jerusalem, 1975 (henceforth: Lexicon), "Balak," pp. 80-81
136 Yoman HaMilhamah, Vol. 2, p. 460 (May 27, 1948).
137 Ibid.p. 459.
138 See: They Flew in the Darkness, pp. 97, 109.
139 See: Wings of Victory, p. 123.

Gardener arranged for the planes to land in the Azores without being searched at a cost of one thousand pounds Sterling in cash, which would be paid by the plane's captain. Two of the B-17s belonged to a non-Jewish American named Charles T. Winters, who had used them for transporting cargoes to Puerto Rico. This fact could make it easier to smuggle the planes out of the United States to Europe.

A B-17 ("Flying Fortress")

At the beginning of June the four Flying Fortresses were ready to fly. The A-20s were still being renovated, and it was therefore decided to leave them behind. On June 12, 1948 the three Flying Fortresses flew out of Miami. The fourth remained behind because of technical difficulties. They arrived in Puerto Rico safely and after refueling they flew on to the Azores. After refueling there, they flew on to Czechoslovakia, arriving in Zatec on June 1, 1948. The planes remained in Czechoslovakia for about a month, during which they were prepared for the role they would be playing, under the supervision of Ray Kurtz. On July 15 orders came to fly the three Flying Fortresses to Israel and along the way to bomb Cairo, El-Arish, and Gaza. That night the planes left on their mission, manned by 17 volunteers from the United States. They carried out their mission successfully.

With the landing of the planes in Ekron that night, the fifth and last flight of the planes purchased in the United States and transported to Israel by air came to an end. The sixth flight was supposed to include the fourth Flying Fortress and the A-20s, but as the A-20s were not yet ready to be flown across, the fourth B-17 left on its own on July 11 from the United States to Canada. The Canadian authorities ordered the crew to fly back to the United States. Ignoring this, the crew flew the plane on to the Azores, where it was transferred to the American authorities. In March 1949 the flight crew was put on trial in the United States and the plane itself was confiscated by the American authorities. On August 25, 1948 United States Customs officials also confiscated the four A-20 planes, which had by that time been repaired. These planes, too, never reached Israel[140].

The importance of the three Flying Fortresses which arrived in the fifth flight was very great. The B-17 was not only a first-class bomber, but also excellent at destroying fighter planes, thanks to the thirteen 0.5 machine guns it was armored with, which could shoot in any direction. These qualities enabled the bomber to fly without the need for a fighter escort.

The Transportation of Planes by Sea

In August 1948, two Mustang P-51s and two Piper Cubs in crates were loaded onto a ship in New York. They arrived in Israel without any problems, and the two Mustangs, immediately after they had been assembled, brought down a British spy plane in Israeli skies. A few weeks later, using the same method, two Hudson planes arrived,

---

140 Ibid.pp. 127-130.

and on October 24, 1948 seventeen Harvard planes were unloaded. In October 1948 two more Mustang P-51s were bought in the United States, along with twenty Steermans and a single Piper Cub. In order to avoid US customs, the planes had been disassembled and the parts sent separately. It was thus possible to describe them as replacement parts, which they were permitted to export. All of these "replacement parts" arrived safely in Israel[141]. The transportation of planes by sea raises a basic question: could these not have been brought in two or three years earlier, and why was this not done?

Mrs. Silverman's Planes

At an Appeal assembly held at the beginning of 1948 in Roanake, Virginia, a Mrs. Silverman mentioned her brother, a former lieutenant-colonel in the United States Air Force, who lived in Paris and dealt with buying and selling used planes. This information was passed on to Hyman Shamir, and as a result a meeting as held between the brother, David Miller, and Freddy Fredkens, a Haganah emissary. This meeting led to the purchase of twenty Norsemen planes for $17,000 apiece from the United States Air Force warehouses in Germany. According to the contract, it was agreed that the planes would be sold with an American license, which meant that they could be flown almost without any limitations. The planes were flown from Germany to Amsterdam for repairs in the KLM workshops, including the fitting of gasoline tanks for long flights. At the end of April 1948 the first three planes were ready. They were flown to Rome, and after being loaded, flew directly to Israel. Their first assignment was to parachute supplies to the beleaguered Gush Etzion. In May and June 1948 some

---

141 Ibid. p. 130.

of the planes were transferred to Israel, but on June 27 the French impounded seven of them, at the demand of the US embassy in Paris to impound any American plane bound for Israel. The other planes were impounded in Holland and Belgium for the same reason. About a month later, all were released and flew to Israel via Czechoslovakia and Yugoslavia. All in all, 17 Norsemen arrived. They were stationed in the Ekron airport and became Wing 35, which was engaged in flying in supplies and in bombing, with most of the crews being Jewish Americans[142].

A Norseman plane

The Quantitative Factor

A summary of the planes acquired in the United States from the beginning of 1948 until the beginning of 1949 shows that during that time period, the following arrived in Israel[143]:

---

142 See: History of the Haganah, Vol. 3, p. 1538; The Trustees, pp. 233-237, 269; Wings of Victory, pp. 133-134; Diary, Vol. 1, p. 407 (May 11, 1948 - the Purchase of 20 Norsemen).
143 See: Wings of Victory, p. 131.

9 Curtiss Commando C-46s (a tenth one exploded in New Mexico)

1 Constellation (2 others were detained in the United States and arrived in Israel after the war)

3 Flying Fortresses (a fourth was confiscated)

4 Mustang P-51s

7 Harvards

20 Steermans

2 Piper Cubs

2 BT-13 trainers

1 Piper

Of 69 planes purchased in the United States, 61 of them arrived in Israel during the War of Independence. In addition, 17 Norsemen were bought from the United States Air Force warehouses in Germany. The total number of planes contributed by American Jewry was 78. In order to estimate the numerical value of the balance of forces, one should compare this to the number of planes in Israel on May 14, 1948, which included but 24 planes, as follows[144]:

Auster 19
Norseman 1
Rapid 1
R.W.D. 1
Bonanza 2
Tailorcraft 1

Numerically, the American contribution meant a growth of 280%. In practice, though, both the technical potential of the planes and the personnel were considerably greater than that. The number of

---

144 Ibid.1.173; similarly Diary, Vol. 1, p. 234 (February 12, 1948).

American volunteers in the Air Force was between 700 and 800 men, about half of all the volunteers who served in the Air Force in the War of Independence[145]. The battle experience of the pilots and other flight crew personnel who were from from the United States was greater and was expressed as well in terms of a qualitative advantage; the American ground personnel were spread throughout all the airports where our planes functioned, from the United States, via Europe, and theirs was a major contribution to the maintenance of the planes and their missions.

The Contribution to the War of Independence

The Balak Operation

When it became clear that the first purchase of arms from the Czechs could not be carried out using the Commando and Constellation planes, a DC4 plane was rented from an American company, and with it the arms were flown from Zatec to an isolated airport in Beit Daras on the night of March 31, 1948. Operation Balak 1 supplied 200 rifles, 40 submachine guns (MG 34), and 150,000 bullets[146], which were distributed that very night to those involved in Operation Nachshon. The added weaponry was essential to the operation, and one should especially appreciate that it took place before the end of the British mandate.

In spite of the protests of the US embassy in Prague about the use of an American airline, Operation Balak continued on May 12, 1948, by means of planes leased from an American corporation. A number

---

145 See: Wings of Victory, p. 295.
146 See: Diary, Vol. 1, p. 331 (March 31, 1948).

of Commando planes which had arrived from the United States were incorporated at the beginning of June into the air transport wing of the Air Force. On May 20, 1948, another 15Messerschmidt 109s were bought from Czechoslovakia, and that day Operation Balak 5 began, which marked a major turning point in the the intensity and extent of the air train from Czechoslovakia to Israel.

By the end of May, four Messerschmidt s had arrived in Israel, and these helped in halting the motorized Egyptian column which came up the northern Shefala coast, toward Tel Aviv. On July 9, the Constellation from Panama landed in Zatec, and joined the air train. The Balak Operations continued until August 12, 1948, at which time the Zatec base was closed, as a result of heavy American pressure on the Czech government. Most of the burden of transporting goods fell on three Commando planes, which worked unceasingly, even though their serviceability kept declining. (Two commando planes exploded - one in New Mexico and one in Ekron on the night of May 20, 1948; a third Commando plane was seized in Rhodes and kept there until the end of the war; two Commando planes were still in Panama; another Commando plane was hit by enemy fire while flying above Yehiam; and the seventh was grounded for repairs).

The Balak Operations included 95 flights, which brought in about 150 tons of equipment, including flying in 25 Messerschmidts, which were carried as cargo by the Commandos and Constellations[147]. The planes, which had originally been meant to bring in the surviving remnant of Jews from Europe to Israel, instead brought in the Czech arms

---

[147] See: Lexicon, pp. 80-81; Wings of Victory, pp. 139-151; The Trustees, pp. 273-274.

shipments, bringing in planes and arms, and these were a significant reinforcement at a very critical time in the War of Independence.

The Avak ("Dust") Operation

During the second cease-fire, the Negev was still cut off from the rest of the country. There was a desperate need to supply it with food immediately, to replace the soldiers there with fresh ones, and to prepare logistically for Operation Yoav.

On August 23, 1948 Leo Gardener, who was now the Operations Officer of the "Transportation Wing" in Ekron, went out to search for a suitable flat area between Ruhama and Shoval. Once one was found, a bulldozer and tractor were brought in, and in the space of three days they prepared a runway for heavy aircraft (Avak 1). Up to the beginning of October that was the only runway open for this operation, and on October 9 a second runway was prepared near Kibbutz Urim (Avak 2). The Avak Operation continued until October 21, and by it 2,224 tons of supplies were moved from the north to the Negev, including 500 tons of gasoline, and more than 270 tons were moved from the Negev to the north. The number of people flown down totaled 1,911, while 5,098 soldiers and civilians were flown north. The Negev Brigade was taken out for reorganization and in its place the Yiftah Brigade was flown in.

We should also add to the accomplishments of the Avak Operation the maintenance of a link to Sedom, which had been cut off. The nature of the runway there was such that only the Norseman planes could land there, and a Norseman squadron, which was set up at the beginning of August, 1948, guaranteed the ability to continue to hold on to besieged Sedom. The commander of the squadron, a Christian American, managed to fly to Sedom five times in a single day.

The Transportation Wing, which had been set up in Ekron based on the purchases from the United States, was the main works contractor for the Avak Operation, aided by Commando, Constellation, Norseman and Dakota planes[148].

Bombing and Aiding Land Forces

The arrival of the Flying Fortresses in Israel marked a crucial turning point in the strength of the Air Force. On July 15, 1948 the area of the king's palace in Cairo was bombed, with 2.5 tons of explosives[149]. In addition, Gaza and Rafiah were bombed (instead of El Arish, as had been the original plan). On July 16 the Flying Fortresses were sent to bomb Damascus. In "the ten day battle," the Air Force dropped 58,300 kilograms of explosives, 48,930 of these delivered by the Flying Fortresses. The air arena extended to Cairo in the south and Damascus in the north, and the Egyptian air force began to lose its superiority.

The B-17s played an active part in all the major operations of the IDF throughout the War of Independence: Yoav, Hiram, Horev, and Uvda. They dropped tens of tons of bombs, assisted the ground forces, and participated in aerial battles. Some of the bombing expeditions also involved the Commandos, which served a dual purpose: transport and bombing. One cannot imagine the success of the Yoav Operation without the success of the Avak Operation and the bombing runs,

---

148 See: Wings of Victory, pp. 224-229, Toledot Milhemet HaKommemiyut (History of the War of Independence), pp. 286-287.
149 See: Diary, Vol. 2, p. 593.

which came to help the Givati brigade. When Ben-Gurion evaluated the contribution of the Air Force in the Yoav Operation, he said:

"We would not have driven out the Egyptian invader and freed the south and the Negev without the Israeli Air Force.[150]"

Ben-Gurion in a B-17

Whereas in the Hiram and Horev Operations the Air Force was primarily involved in bombing and aerial combat, in the Uvda Operation the transportation planes again were active participants. In the first three days of the operation, tens of tons of equipment were moved from Ekron to Sdei Avraham for the Negev and Golani brigades. The flights to Sdei Avraham and Eilat to transport equipment continued even after the conclusion of the operation[151].

---

150 See: Wings of Victory, p. 255.
151 Ibid.pp. 234-289.

The acquisition of the planes in the United States came at a most critical time of the War of Independence - the invasion by the Arab countries on May 15, 1948. The planes, along with the Mahal foreign volunteers from the United States, were the primary basis for the Israeli Air Force. The volunteers' dedication and professionalism, combined with the air force's ability to supply transportation, to engage in bombing, and its achievement of air superiority, were decisive in the great victory of the War of Independence.

The co-pilot Abraham Goldreich and his friends with B-17 aircraft

The very high value of the United States planes in the War of Independence raises and emphasizes the following questions:

Why was the purchase of planes so haphazard in the beginning?

Why weren't these purchases planned for at a much earlier stage, as was the case with machinery?

Could these purchases have been made earlier?

The Ships

As opposed to the haphazard way in the buying of planes, the purchase of ships had a clearly defined purpose, with a long tradition going back to the beginning of the 1930s. During World War II the "illegal immigration" was concentrated in the hands of the "Mossad LeAliyah Bet" (the "Institute for Level 2 - i.e., 'illegal' - Immigration") headed by Shaul Avigur. The "Mossad" set up an extensive system of contacts, which was activated with great intensity from the end of 1945 until the establishment of the State. The factor leading to the setting up of a center in the United States to buy ships was the desire to move from small ships which could carry tens of people to large ships which could carry thousands. Between August 1945 and June 1948 the Mossad sent 64 ships to Palestine/Israel, plus two ships of the Etzel, the "Ben Hecht" and the "Altalena." The number of "illegal immigrants" which arrived during that time was about 70,000[152].

During that time, with the aid of the Sonneborn Institute, 18 ships were bought in the United States[153] and four more through the Committee (two of which never sailed; see Note 75 of Chapter 2). In terms of the number of ships, the Jews of the United States thus contributed 30%. As opposed to this, in terms of the number of "illegal immigrants" brought in by these ships, the number was more than 50%. Among the large ships purchased by the Mossad in the United States were the President Warfield, which became known as the Exodus, and sailed

---

152 See: Mordechai Naor, HaHa'apalah ("the Illegal Immigration"), Ministry of Defense Publ., Tel Aviv, 1978 (henceforth: "the Illegal Immigration"), pp. 144-145, Appendix A; similarly: Oniyot O Medinah (Ships or a State) (henceforth: Ships or a State), pp33,18-19
153 See: The Trustees, p. 41.

from France in July 1947 with 4,530 "illegal immigrants," as well as the Pan York and the Pan Crescent (which were renamed the Kibbutz Galuyot and Atzma'ut respectively), which sailed in June 1948 with 15,239 "illegal immigrants.[154]"

The preparation of these large ships to carry thousands of people meant the supplying of fantastic quantities of food and required exacting administrative planning. This was done with the cooperation of communal Zionist institutions. Thus, for example, the Jewish community in Philadelphia organized a major social and entertainment evening in a luxurious hall. For this, announcements were printed and invitations sent out, and at the event itself they announced loudly who had pledged what, and that added to the amount pledged. An event of that kind was against all the rules of secrecy and carried the danger of revealing their plans[155].

While the acquisition of these ships had only one purpose - "illegal immigration" - it nevertheless, indirectly, and without any prior planning, served to prepare a Jewish naval force for the War of Independence. In spite of the dependence of the Yishuv on the sea lanes, there had never been a conception of the military implications and the immediate and future needs of the Israeli navy. Both in the mandatory era and during the War of Independence it was by sea that most immigrants, raw materials, foodstuffs, oil, machinery, and equipment arrived. The conclusion of the Mandate accentuated the need for an Israeli navy, which could protect the movement of ships sailing to the new state and would be able to act both defensively and offensively against the Arab navies.

---

154 See: "The Illegal Immigration," pp. 144-145.
155 See: Ships or a State, p. 41.

From the beginning of 1948 discussions were held and proposals voiced regarding the acquisition of naval vessels and the establishment of a navy. In January 1948 three proposals were made: one from a member of the merchant marine, which suggested the establishment of a naval border patrol; the second by Captain Miller, which dealt with a naval defense program; and the third by Bar-Kochba Meyerowitz, which was based on the second proposal and expanded it into an attack force against naval blockade[156].

Following the announcement by Yigael Yadin on February 5, 1948, head of Operations Branch of the Haganah, that subjugated the naval forces to the authority of the land forces, Ben-Gurion wrote on February 18, 1948 to Yadin:

> The naval defense is the decisive one in the defensive realm, and there is need within the General Staff for a naval branch and for a special naval force. I am now working with experts in clarifying what tools are needed for this. In the past, the naval service was directed primarily to **"illegal immigration"**. This purpose still stands as before, **but the task of supplying security requires a new and fundamental effort, and the available tools are not up to this.**
>
> As a result, I do not accept your directive on directing volunteers to service in the navy to the Bulgarian Brigade (a code name for the

---

156 See: Eliezer Tal, Mivtza'ei Hayl HaYam BeMilhemet HaKomemiyut (The Operations of the Navy in the War of Independence) (henceforth: Operations of the Navy), Ma'arakhot, 1964, pp. 50-54. See also: Diary, Vol. 1, p. 251 (February 18, 1948 - "the Meirowitz and Ze'ev HaYam Plan).

Palmah), but rather **we must set up a special naval force which is subject directly to the General Staff and the High Command**[157].

The discussions regarding the establishment of a special naval force went on for about a month. The Palmah Command was opposed to such a structure of the naval force. Its view was that such a force should be under the Palmah Command. The order which Yadin issued on March 17, 1948 brought an end to the debate[158].

The new Command began to act, among others, to acquire naval vessels abroad and to recruit professionals. The date for the final determination regarding the establishment of a naval force which would be subject to the General Staff, whose aims and tasks, beyond bringing in immigrants, came so late that there was no time to purchase anything. On May 15, a number of serious threats came from the Egyptians: a) a sea blockade; b) attacks on the Haifa and Tel Aviv ports; c) the shelling of the coastline; d) landings; e) aid to the land forces. Due to these threats, there was an immediate need to initiate a naval attack force, and the only possible way to do so was to refit some of the "illegal immigrant" ships as warships. The liberation of Haifa on April 28, 1948 gave them the real possibility of commencing the process.

The "illegal immigrant" ships, which had been bought in the United States after World War II from United States Navy surplus, became the first-line ships of the Israeli Navy, and due to the relatively late time at which the State of Israel defined its naval needs, these ships were the

---

157 See: Operations of the Navy, pp. 55-56 (my emphasis). Similarly, Diary, Vol. 1, p. 295.
158 See: Diary, Vol. 1, pp. 275, 288, 294, 295.

ones used in the battles, carrying the naval struggle continuously and diligently until the end of the war.

The "Illegal Immigration" Ships

a. The "Eilat" A-16. This ship had been an ice-breaker in the United States navy during World War II. It was purchased by the Mossad in the United States in 1946, renamed Medinat HaYehudim, and brought 2,664 "illegal immigrants" from Bulgaria and Romania. In October 1947 it was seized by the British and docked at the Haifa port. Its good technical condition enabled it to enter service on May 21, 1948, but its slow speed, its nature and its armaments restricted its use to escorting other ships and guarding the coastline.

b. The 'Wedgewood" - K-18. A Canadian Korvette which had been bought by the Mossad in the United States in 1946. This ship brought 1,257 people to the country from Italy in June 1946. It was seized by the British at the end of that month and docked at the Haifa port. The ship had excellent maneuverability and armaments, which made it an attack vessel. It was used for patrols, for guarding the coast, for escort duties, and for actions against enemy ships and coasts.

c. The "Haganah" - K-20. A Korvette which was the twin of the Wedgewood, and bought in the United States along with the Wedgewood. In July 1946 it brought in 2,678 people from Yugoslavia and Italy. It was seized by the British at the end of that month and docked at the Haifa port. It required a relatively lengthy period of time to make it seaworthy, and only on July 18, 1948 was it able to sail. Its tasks were the same as those of the Wedgewood. One should note that these two ships were the most battle-ready in the entire Israeli navy.

d. The "HaTikvah" - K-22. This was an antiquated type of the United States P.C. patrol ships. It was bought in the United States in May 1947 and brought in 1,414 people from Italy, was seized that month, and docked at the Haifa port. It went into service on June 9, 1948, but shortly thereafter it was found not to be suitable for the navy, and it was therefore transferred in July 1948 to the "Mossad for Immigration Level 2."

e. The "Maoz" - K-24. This ship was bought in the United States by the Committee for Etzel in 1947. It was renamed the Avrieli and then named the Ben Hecht. In March 1947 it brought 600 immigrants from France and that month it was seized by British. Its refurbishment began in July 1948 and was only completed in September that year. Its speed, and various other features it had, made it the mother-ship for demolition engineers, and that was its main contribution in the war. In this capacity, it was involved in the sinking of the Egyptian "King Farouk." In addition, it was involved in patrols, escorting ships, and guarding the beaches[159].

The Acquisition of Ships and Naval Equipment for the Navy

Yehudah Arazi's attempts to buy a landing craft in the United States did not stem from plans for the future needs of the navy, but from

---

159 This is a placeholder.

the desire to utilize the large capacity of such a craft, which could be used to transport a very large quantity of equipment to Israel on the day the British left the country - a type of miniature D-Day. This idea received the support and encouragement of Ben-Gurion, and meshed with "Plan D.[160]" This was expressed as well in the search for LCTs (Landing Craft Tanks) which would move under cover of torpedo boats. On February 8, 1948, Ben-Gurion wrote in his diary[161]:

> We want to bring a number of ships in the middle of May - for defense against an attack by sea. We should buy 4,000 ton LCTs - "invasion boats" - and alongside them torpedo boats which they sell in America, without torpedoes. Instead of torpedoes, they should install machine guns and small cannon. An LCT costs $45,000. Each boat (without torpedoes) costs $6000 - $7500 ... [Shind] proposes that we take Paul Schulman for this job ... I conveyed to him [Shind] the decision of the Executive - [giving preference to] the "illegal immigration" of capable young men for work and defense, and not general immigration (children and old people) ... He should direct every action toward training young people for defense of the country for D-Day [the day we are invaded] ... Eliyahu [Sakharov] is leaving for America tomorrow ... I told him to work on acquiring LCTs - large and small, and fast motor boats.

Arazi's attempt to buy the large LCT "A.A.H. Auto" for use by the Haganah, which had begun in December 1947, ultimately failed. Even

---
160 See: Diary, Vol. 1, p. 147.
161 Ibid.pp. 215-216 (February 8, 1948).

though the ship was bought for $125,000 and another $5000 were invested in repairs and legal arrangements, complications regarding the repayment of the amount owed for the purchase of the ship went to court, which then issued a stop order, preventing the ship from sailing from the United States. In April 1948 it was clear that the deal had failed. The ship was broken up and sold to a scrap merchant who was one of the members of the Institute[162].

Sakharov, who had been assigned the task of buying landing craft, also failed in his mission, and the plan to have landing craft ready by May 15 was never realized.

The conclusion of the deliberations about establishing a naval branch, which had ended in March 1948, was the demand to appoint professional buyers outside Palestine. As a result, Paul Schulman and Joseph Harel began working in the United States[163].

It was impossible to remove military vessels from this country, as they were considered to be military equipment. It was possible, though, to overcome this difficulty by working with Panamanian, Honduran and other companies. The ships that were bought also needed repairs, and they were therefore sent to France - via Mexico or another country in South America. Another problem was the need to find experienced crew members. The practical and legal problems led to a long delay in the acquisition activities.

---

162 See: The Trustees, pp. 117-122, 226-227.
163 "HaRekhesh BeArHaB" (Arms Acquisition in the United States), IDF Archive, File 51
     See also: Operations of the Navy, pp. 224-229.

"Ramat Rahel"

The attempts at acquiring naval vessels by Victor (Vic) Avronin between March and May 1948 failed. On May 21 orders were issued from Israel to transfer the responsibility for buying naval equipment to David Nameri, the representative of the Mossad LeAliyah (the "Immigration Institute"). With Nameri's appointment, the purchasing requirements also changed, following the decision to transfer the "illegal immigration" ships to the navy fleet. When it was understood that the navy now had two Korvettes - the Haganah and the Wedgewood - the decision was made to purchase fast ocean vessels. In the orders sent on May 31 to the delegation in the United States, these stated: "We need fast vessels - 8-16 knots - because meanwhile we have obtained other powerful vessels. We no longer need tugs.[164"]

Similarly, orders were given to buy sea cannon for the existing ships.

On June 8, a patrol boat (P.C.) was bought, which was later named the Noga. It left for Mexico and from there to Marseilles. It arrived there on August 28, was delayed for repairs, and arrived in Israel on September 30, 1948[165].

In July 1948 new orders emanated from Israel, whereby - among others - they needed 6-8 torpedo ships. Two invasion ships - P-51, Ramat Rahel, and M-53, Nitzanim - left the United States on November 23, 1948 for Marseilles, and from there to Israel. Both arrived at the end of December 1948. Following negotiations to buy torpedo ships, one of these sailed to Cuba, and from there, on December 12, 1948, to Israel, towed there by another ship. Unfortunately, this ship sank off the coast of Sicily.

On October 12, a contract was signed in New York to purchase three frigates which would be transferred in Marseilles. The first arrived in Haifa on February 21, 1949, the second on April 28, and the third in May. Three motorboats had arrived from the United States between August and December 1948, as gifts to the Israeli navy: M-43, M-47, and M-49. In addition to all of these, motors, various replacement parts, communications gear, radar, uniforms, training manuals, etc., were bought for the navy[166].

Of all the purchases made in the United States on behalf of the Israeli Navy during the War of Independence, only the Noga (K-26)

---

164 Ibid.p. 227. See also: IDF Archive, 2851/50, File 64 - Letter from the Head of Naval Operations to the Representative of the Navy in the United States.
165 See: Operations of the Navy, p. 228.
166 Ibid.p. 228.

was actually involved in the war, and even its involvement was very minimal, because of technical problems with its motors. The attempts during that time to purchase items for the navy from the United States ran into all types of problems. Beyond the political limitations there was a lack of coordination between the High Command in Israel and those involved in trying to make purchases. The budget was limited, there was a lack of clarity as to what was actually needed and what was available in the United States, and - more than anything else - the decision to embark on these purchases came at a very late stage.

"Noga"

The Contribution During the War of Independence

One may regard the shelling of Tyre on July 18, 1948 as the beginning of the Israeli Navy's actions in the War of Independence. This action was carried out by the Wedgewood and the Eilat, and more than anything one may regard this as a demonstration of the existence of the Israeli Navy and its ability to act[167].

The sinking of the Leno on April 9, 1948 in the port of Bari in Italy by Haganah demolition experts did not prevent the transfer of its munitions to the Argiro three months later. On August 26, 1948 the Wedgewood and Eilat forced the Argiro to stop in the middle of the ocean and seized all the munitions which had been meant for Syria (the Shalal 3 Operation). On August 29 these munitions arrived in Haifa[168].

"Argiro"

---

167 Ibid.pp. 120-122.
168 Ibid.pp. 123-137.

In October 1948 a new stage began in the activities of the Navy. Coordination between the land forces and the Navy became concrete and in the Yoav Operation the actions of the Egyptian Navy on the Gazan coast were disrupted. Whereas until October 1948 there were constant ties between the Egyptian Navy and the Gaza Strip, from the end of October the Egyptian Navy stopped any oceanic transportation to the Gaza Strip.

On October 22, the Emir Farouk and the mine sweeper B.Y.M.S. were sunk in a bold operation of the naval demolitions unit, which was aided by the Maoz (K-24), which served as the mother ship for this venture. The power and accomplishments of the Navy in the Yoav Operation had an influence not only in the sea arena: a few weeks after the operation, the world maritime insurance companies in England and the United States lowered the naval insurance premiums to Israel, which had been raised 50% at the beginning of the war[169].

"Eilat"

---

169 Ibid.pp. 148-170.

On December 17, 1948 the Egress, docked in the Beirut port, was damaged. The action was carried out by a demolitions unit which had come from the mother ship, the Palmah (M-19), where the Eilat (K-20) served as an escort and cover, and to assist those who carried out the operation (Operation David[170]).

In the Horev Operation, the Navy was able to impose a blockade on the Gaza Strip, and throughout that operation not a single enemy ship reached the coast; nor was there any sea transportation along its entire coast. The shelling of the Strip caused Egypt to remove a sizable quantity of cannon, searchlights and patrols from the coast. The shelling created a feeling among the Egyptians of covering fire preceding an invasion, and that caused the enemy forces to remain in place[171]. The acquisition of "illegal immigration" ships in 1946 and 1947, and the acquisition of ships for the Navy in 1948, gave the navy the primary basis for its operation. We should add to this the contribution of those American Jews who gave of their battle, command, and organizational experience, headed by Paul Schulman, who was the first commander of the Navy. It is true that in the War of Independence the Israeli Navy did not vanquish the Egyptian Navy, but it succeeded in preventing the enemy from exploiting the war on the ocean as a factor to win the overall war. This aim was achieved in full, and thus this can this be seen as a strategic victory.

Other Equipment

Communications Equipment

In January 1948 Yaakov Janowski ("Jan") left for the United States by Ben-Gurion's order, to undertake the purchase of a massive amount

---

170 Ibid.pp. 171-176.
171 Ibid.pp. 177-200.

of communications equipment. Equipment valued at a quarter of a million dollars and weighing 250 tons was bought[172], and it arrived in Palestine at the end of March, 1948. This included: five radars; the equipment to set up twelve large radio stations - AM/FRCL; 1,000 telephones; 200 switchboards for 6 and 12 lines; 800 miles of phone lines; laboratory equipment; 12 receivers; generators; 900 small walkie-talkies (MaB); 100 ScR units on the 30 and 40 wavelengths; 70 608-1508 units on the 20-40 wavelengths; 10 Motorola units; and thousands of replacement parts[173]. We must add to this the hundreds of units sent by Dani Fliderblum and which had been concealed in "production machinery." This acquisition in the United States enabled them to set up powerful radio stations in the European capitals.

The ties between the Political Department of the Jewish Agency and the United States and London were reorganized. Kol Yisrael, the radio broadcast service, was able to transmit with much greater power, broadcasting from secret locations in the Givat Brenner and Ramat HaKhovesh areas. The first broadcast of the Israeli government, on the night of May 15, 1948, was transmitted to the world via 48 radio stations in the United States.

---

[172] See: Diary, Vol. 1, p. 303 (March 13, 1948). Similarly, Arkhion Toledot HaHaganah (Archive of the History of the Haganah), Document No. 4955.
[173] See: Diary, Vol. 1, pp. 288, 337.

The demolitions team which sank the "Emir Farouk," with Ben-Gurion. From left to right: Z. Abramov, Y. Bin-Nun, Y. Ritov, D. Ben-Gurion, Y. Vardi, Y. Brookman, Chief of Staff Y. Dori

From its very beginning, the IDF's communications network was based on US equipment. As "Jan" noted when reserve American officers visited the country in April/May 1948, they were astounded at the modern equipment with with they were familiar in their own army. According to these experts, the IDF units just before and after the founding of the State were equipped no worse than the British army in World War II[174].

Maintenance

On March 28, 13 of 50 half-tracks which had been purchased by the "Materials for Palestine" organization, ostensibly for agricultural purposes, arrived in the country. The remaining half-tracks only arrived at the end of 1948[175].

---

174 See: Arkhion Toledot HaHaganah (Archive of the History of the Haganah), Document No. 4955, p. 4.
175 See: History of the Haganah, Vol. 3, p. 1533.

The activities of "Materials for Palestine" were focused primarily on collecting and sending those items which would equip an army, from the individual soldier and up. The Jewish Hatmakers Union in the United States manufactured thousands of caps just for the IDF[176]. The fund-raising campaign of Golda Meir in the United States in February 1948 netted about 50 million dollars and increased the number of those ready to engage in voluntary activities such as those of Materials for Palestine[177].

The ship Flying Arrow, which left New York on February 26, 1948, carried 350,000 sandbags; 10,000 wool blankets; 10,000 helmets; 12 first aid station kits; 33 crates of medical operation equipment; 4 water purification systems; and one milling machine.

That was the first shipment by Materials for Palestine[178].

"Wedgewood"

---

176 See: BaDerekh LeTzahal (On the Way to the IDF), Ma'arakhot, Tel Aviv, 1977 (henceforth: On the Way to the IDF), p. 292.
177 See: Ben-Gurion, Vol. 2, p. 674. Similarly, Golda Meir, Hayyai (My Life), Sifri'at Ma'ariv, Tel Aviv, 1975, pp. 155-157.
178 See: The Trustees, p. 162.

The Commitment

On February 27, the A.K. Almar Blumqvist sailed from Los Angeles with a cargo of 350 large tents; 1,700 helmets; and 2,000 helmet liners[179].

The demand for fortification equipment intensified after the preparation of the Joshua Plan (named after Joshua Globerman), which the Haganah Executive carried out in January 1948 and which was the first attempt to plan the defense of the country against the invasion by regular and irregular armies of the Arab states. "Plan D," which was adapted in March 1948 was the conclusion of the Joshua Operation[180].

"Haganah"

The increased demands from the country, Golda Meir's trip to the United States and the intensification of the battles, all of these brought about greater activity of Materials for Palestine assisted by the members of the Institute, who worked intensively throughout the United States in collecting equipment: Chicago sent 100 bales of barbed wire (and offered 11 tons of camouflage paint). New Jersey sent 25,000 helmets;

---
179 Ibid.p. 162.
180 See: BaDerekh LeTzahal (On the Way to the IDF), p. 273.

Ohio sent 92,000 parachutes; earth merchants in Indiana and Brooklyn sent 250,000 sandbags; St. Paul, Minnesota sent two mine detectors (and offered 600 more); Miami sent five anti-aircraft searchlights and generators; a group of discharged soldiers in New York organized the purchase of thirty field binoculars - by US government regulations, each soldier was permitted to buy one. In San Francisco, 14,000 helmets were collected, along with 3,600 meters of netting cloth; 2,500 kit bags; four large rolls of copper cable; and three large crates of communications gear. Philadelphia sent a mobile hospital; Detroit sent generators, machinery, and a machine to ascertain octane proof. Kansas City sent helmets, folding beds, spades, sheets, and nurses' uniforms. Birmingham supplied steel plates. Augusta, Georgia sent cases for revolvers and compasses. Baltimore supplied jeep covers, communications gear, maps, sextants, and binoculars for the navy.

Large quantities of uniforms and other clothing were collected. The demands of the Haganah for vehicles brought about the shipping of many vehicles, including jeeps, tow trucks, ambulances, cars, replacement parts, and field equipment[181].

At the beginning of May a hundred sharpshooter binoculars, along with chemicals, which had been gathered during the mission of Ephraim Katzir to the United States, were sent[182].

In March 1948 the heads of the Executive in Palestine formulated the idea of importing food from abroad in order to alleviate the drain on the maintenance budget in the country. Materials for Palestine thus got involved in buying preserved meat, milk, and fish, flour and other foodstuffs, to supply the Yishuv for an extended amount of time.

---

181 See: The Trustees, pp. 162-165.
182 See: Diary, Vol. 1, p. 413 (May 13, 1948).

Up to December 1948 three million dollars' worth of food had been bought[183].

In the second half of 1948 and the beginning of 1949 the activities of Materials for Palestine reached their peak. Between August 1948 and January 1949 hundreds of tons of all types of equipment were sent to Israel by ship, along with the crates of disassembled planes as "replacement parts." According to what Teddy Kolleck told Ben-Gurion on December 19, 1948: "They are collecting gifts to the army at a rate of one and a half million dollars a month, and this can be doubled[184]..."

There is no doubt that the purchasing activities in the United States were the most vital and essential artery in keeping the IDF supplied during the War of Independence.

Hank Greenspun and the arms deals in Hawaii and Mexico

In February 1948 Hank Greenspun and Willy Sosnow left for Honolulu, Hawaii, in order to investigate the possibility of purchasing arms from the giant army surplus warehouses there. The purchase they made included 400 0.3 machine guns, about 20 0.5 machine guns, and about 80 AR-2800 motors for Commando planes[185].

On March 11, 1948, 58 crates were loaded onto the deck of the A.K. Line Victor, addressed to Schwimmer Air Service, and left for Wilmington in California. The merchandise was hidden in Los Angeles with the help of Bernard Fineman, and a few weeks later it was sent by sea to Acapulco, Mexico, on the Idyllia, which had been leased by Greenspun.

---

183 Ibid.Vol. 1, pp. 311, 321; and so too Vol. 3, p. 859.
184 Ibid.Vol. 3, pp. 881-882, 886.
185 See: Wings of Victory, p. 111; The Trustees, pp. 174-180.

In April 1948 Hyman Shamir and Eliyahu Sakharov initiated secret contacts with the Mexican government in order to make a large purchase of arms, including P-47 planes, Sherman tanks, and 75 mm. cannon. The deal was carried out to a certain extent in August 1948. After Al Schwimmer paid about $260,000 to the Mexican government, the ship Kaplus[186] was loaded up with 36 French 75 mm. howitzers, 17,000 shells, 2,000 air bombs, 7 million bullets, and about 500 machine guns and sub-machine guns, including those which Greenspun had obtained in Hawaii, and which had been brought to Hawaii on the yacht Idyllia. In addition to this cargo, barrels of aviation fuel were loaded, as well as 1400 tons of sugar on top of the arms, as camouflage, should the British stop the ship in Gibraltar[187].

The Kaplus arrived in Israel in September 1948, The cannon purchase was not particularly successful, but as opposed to that, the aviation fuel made the air force participation in Avak Operation and the Yoav Operation possible[188].

Bernard Fineman managed to arrange in Los Angeles the purchase of 15 medium M-4 tanks, which were sent to Houston by train. The tanks were supposed to be loaded onto a Mexican ship, but in the end they stayed in the United States[189].

One should add to all the quantities of arms which were purchased another 300 bazookas and many tons of explosives and gunpowder[190].

---

186 See: The Trustees, pp. 174-180.
187 See: The Trustees, pp. 271-272.
188 See: Toledot Milhemet HaKommemiyut (History of the War of Independence), p. 289
189 See: The Trustees, p. 157.
190 See: Ben-Gurion, Yoman HaMilhamah (The War Diary), Vol. 1, pp. 86, 219.

In taking into account the overall picture, the amount of arms purchased in the United States was relatively little when compared to the arms acquisition in Europe. But if we add to that quantity the production of the "machinery" which had been bought in the United States, the contribution of the purchases in this country were central. In spite of this, we cannot avoid the question whether it was possible to send much more from the United States.

Hillel Kook (Peter Bergson)

Chapter 4:

Why was the US Potential not Utilized to the Fullest?

The Human Resources

The establishment of the Sonneborn Institute was like a display of a lack of confidence in the ability of the official Zionist institutions to participate in the organizational and active burden of establishing a secret purchasing system and of running it. Ben-Gurion's initiative in establishing the Institute also implied that he had a positive feeling about the collective response of the large Jewish community of the United States. The thousands of Jews who were ultimately involved in the different activities served to ensure the success of the purchasing system in the United States. Had there not been this positive mass response, there is no doubt that the purchasing system in this country would have suffered a resounding defeat. On the other hand, one is able to understand the limited response of the official Jewish institutions to the work of Zaslani at the end of World War II given the background of the policy of the US government, their fear of dual loyalty, and the long diaspora tradition which had created a mentality of a minority without any feeling of self-pride.

At the same time, there is no doubt that the activities of the Zionist organizations in the United States underwent a revolution during that era. The charismatic leadership of Abba Hillel Silver as president of the American Zionist Organization signified a new line in the political activities of the Zionist institutions. The open and forceful demand of the Truman administration to express positive support of the establishment of a Jewish state, and for a solution to the problem of the Displaced Persons utilizing the media to influence public opinion, Members of Congress and the members of the administration, provided large numbers of American Jews with legitimation to become involved in the secret arms acquisitions, even though this was sometimes patently illegal. Among the American Jews there were those who drew a parallel between the struggle of the United States to achieve its independence and that of the Jews to establish a Jewish state. Thus, for example, when Leonard Weissman was detained for having been involved in the purchase of arms and in the concealment of explosives, he said: "Had Marquis Lafayette not helped the United States acquire arms when we fought for our independence, we might not have emerged victorious, and no one criticized Eamon de-Valera when he came to this country for that very cause.[191"]

Weissman's statement was the motivation of the Jews who participated in these underground activities. These activities gave them a feeling of

---

191 See: The Trustees, p. 147.

conspiracy and heroism, which stemmed, among others, from their reaction to the helplessness they had felt in trying to save the Jews of Europe. The comparison with the struggle of the United States for its independence was made in order to grant moral legitimation to actions which were illegal, while at the same time to emphasize and clarify their identification with America, as required by their American citizenship. The very low percentage of Jews who immigrated to Palestine from the United States[192] is an indication of this, where their actions on behalf of the State of Israel were carried out without impinging on their profound basic loyalty to the United States.

The conflict between the American Jews' desire to maintain their loyalty to the United States and the need to violate the law forced the heads of the purchasing delegation in the United States to have Palestinians run the operational cells - especially at the beginning. As the activities expanded, and along with them the organizational framework, more and more American "trustees" were brought in. Whereas at the outset the initiative had come primarily from the Haganah leaders, as the number of Americans involved grew, the internal initiatives grew apace. It was but natural that those who were intimately acquainted with the American milieu and conditions should also map out the paths to be followed (such as setting up fictitious companies and attending to the legal matters involved), and would increase their influence and take the initiative as they were granted a greater scope within which to work.

The intensification in the arms acquisition process was in direct proportion to the number of American Jews who were involved in

---

[192] See: Marshall Sklar, Yehudei Artzot HaBrit (The Jews of the United States), Am Oved, Tel Aviv, 1972.

it, despite the innate contradiction of the very character of secret, compartmentalized work. The question to be asked is whether bringing Americans actively into the picture at an earlier time than they were actually brought in might not have increased productivity.

The Sonneborn Institute began functioning about a year after the meeting with Ben-Gurion, which took place on July 1, 1945. Dori's delegation was active for all of 1946 and the first half of 1947, working methodically, thoroughly and secretly to enlist supporters throughout the United States. Reuven Dafni notes in his interview that the meetings generally took place in private homes and in very small gatherings[193]. This method worked well in recruiting trustworthy individuals, but precious time was wasted. By 1944, the ground was ready for kick-starting the process. The war had not yet been concluded, and the United States was furnishing its allies with phenomenal quantities of armaments under the provisions of Lend-Lease. American Jewry had begun to understand the terrible fate of the European Jews, and most of all - in the United States itself there was a war atmosphere. Such an atmosphere is familiar to Israelis as well: the supervision within the country is more lax, the bureaucracy tends to cut corners; all devote themselves to a single task - victory - and ignore procedures which under normal circumstances would have needed to be followed in full. Zaslani's activities were meant to start the process, but in reality one should regard them as a preliminary scouting out of the territory in order to learn the problems. Ideally, this type of work should have been completed by 1944.

The end of the war would have been the most appropriate time to recruit Jewish-American soldiers and to examine the possibilities

---

193 See: Reuven Dafni, Interview, Yad Vashem, June 13, 1985.

and needs of establishing a Jewish army. Colonel David ("Mickey") Marcus, who arrived in Palestine in February 1948, presented Ben-Gurion at the beginning of March1948 with a comprehensive report about the condition of the Haganah[194].

Had this study been carried out two years earlier, it is possible that it would have avoided doctrinal disagreements which arose in the Haganah in 1947, and would certainly have contributed to the formulation of aims and goals regarding the acquisition of arms in the United States. In a letter to Moshe Sharett and Golda Myerson (Meir) on March 3, 1948, Ben-Gurion wrote: "Again, send us ten Marcuses, a few naval officers, pilots - and pray that the equipment should arrive.[195]"

From that perspective, valuable time had been lost ,which resulted in but a partial utilization of American Jewry. The following words of Teddy Kolleck regarding Marcus indicate the internal conflicts which arose among the members of the Haganah in accepting outside advice, while at the same time indicated the problem that Marcus faced in trying to find a common language with them:

The position of many of our underground fighters was: "These officers, who are experts at shiny buttons and belts, what do they know?" It took some time before "our" British soldiers could

---

194 See: Ben-Gurion, Diary, Vol. 1, pp. 273-274.
195 Ibid.p. 276. See too: Yoav Gelber, Lama Pirku et HaPalmah? (Why did they Dismantle the Palmah?), Schocken, Jerusalem and Tel Aviv, p. 37: "We do not have the personnel to train officers. The trainers do not have enough experience - i.e., exercises. We are able to offer theoretical instruction to the platoon commanders, but we cannot give them the opportunity to lead a platoon. We should send a hundred men overseas ... We do not have teachers for a command school. We should send the platoon commanders to France for a few months, primarily for maneuvers." See also: p. 39 (Sneh's comment): "There are none in Palestine who can run a school and people should be sent abroad."

influence them. The irregular forces of the Haganah and the Palmah represented the majority of the army.

On his first visit to the country, Mickey (Marcus) found a common language with them **more quickly** than did those of our personnel who had been in the ranks of the British army[196].

There is no doubt that understanding the potential contained within American Jewry and linking it to the needs of the Haganah at an earlier time would have made a significant contribution to the expansion of the arms acquisition.

Concept and Theory

What Ben-Gurion had said in 1939 about the need to establish a Jewish army was understood by most of the members of the Executive as a direct translation of the territorial threat to Palestine itself. The possible threat of invasion by the Arab armies was not taken into account at all at that time. In 1945, Ben-Gurion already spoke about the two threats. His words were expressed both in his meeting with the seventeen Jews at the Sonneborn home and at the National Executive of the Haganah:

> The structure of the Haganah force, as it was assessed and established in accordance with the General Staff order of June 1945, stemmed from the danger of an attack on the Jewish Yishuv primarily by the Arabs of Palestine. The danger of an attack of the country by the neighboring Arab countries, as was revealed

---

196 See: Yerushalayim Ahat (One Jerusalem), p. 94 (my emphasis).

during this time, requires a different structure and preparation. Faced by regular armies, it is necessary to prepare a military force - trained, armed, and structured as a military force[197].

The great failure of Ben-Gurion was his inability to instill belief among others of his chilling forecast and the conclusions which needed to be drawn from this. It is true that he had their esteem, but his involvement in defense matters was regarded as unrealistic and lacking any professional basis. Despite the "Seminar" between March and September 1947 which Ben-Gurion underwent, the heads of the Haganah did not regard him as an authority in defense matters, and his forecast of the invasion by the Arab armies was regarded as the nightmare of an old man who was more than sixty years old, who had never been involved personally in any military activity of any kind.

Elhanan Yishai mentioned a meeting between Ben-Gurion and the heads of the Haganah in the summer of 1947:

> They spoke about their conception regarding the developments in the future. When they spoke of arms, they mentioned arms that were appropriate for platoons, squads: of course, no one spoke of supporting fire. He paid attention and listened, and suddenly he asked: "And cannon? And planes?"

At first, there was silence in the room. People looked at one another and soft whispering began. A few had to hold themselves back from laughing aloud. He went outside for a while. "He's crazy," a number of those present exclaimed. "What's he talking about? We are talking

---

197 See: Sefer Todelot HaHaganah (The Book of the History of the Haganah), Vol. 3, Appendix 46, p. 1948.

about Sten guns and rifles, and he is dreaming about cannon and planes." One of those higher-ups who was present at the meeting said simply: "I think that the Old Man (as he was known) has simply lost his mind!" The "Old Man" came back into the room and continued where he had left off. He began laying out his conception of what we were to expect. "There will be a war," he said. "The Arab states will be united and will jointly fight us. There will be a battle front. It will no longer be the fight of a squad or a platoon. We have to establish a modern army. We have to think of the means of a modern army." There was total silence in the hall, and he, as was usual for him, repeated himself time and again[198].

At the meeting of the Zionist Executive in Zurich that year, Ben-Gurion was faced by a failure to understand his message. In his memoirs, he wrote:

> One could not feel any fear about the danger of the Arab invasion of the neighboring countries. My attempt to place this question as the center of our concern ... failed[199].

The disturbances of 1936 brought about the development of a theory of guerrilla warfare within the Haganah. The tactical and operational thought indeed assumed a more active character, but the strategic plan remain passive. The essence of the theoretical development was that their numerical weakness had to be concealed by moving the forces around in the field, in accordance with Yitzchak Sadeh's theory:

> Our strength will not be measured by either quantity or fire power. Where it is impossible to engage in a frontal attack, one must know

---

198 See: Ben-Gurion, Vol. 2, p. 657.
199 See: BaDerekh LeTzava uMedinat Yisrael (On the Way to the Army and the State of Israel), a series of articles in Davar, Article No. 57, September 1964.

how to maneuver, to find weak points in the enemy's system, to act against the transportation lines of the enemy ... Our military thinking was not conventional. We always took into account that the enemy would be stronger than us, both in manpower and in fire power, and we could not have a decisive victory purely in terms of physical power, but needed to maneuver and to act against the enemy's weak points[200].

In accordance with this theory, the Haganah members came up with solutions of peripheral defense around settlements and strategic key points, while using local tactical attacks within a comprehensive defensive strategy.

The emphasis in the training of the fighters and commanders of the Haganah was focused on initiative, resourcefulness, and original thought. Within this framework, the equipment and arms available occupied a secondary role. Therefore, the meaning of the establishment of a Jewish army was understood by most commanders of the Haganah and the Palmah as the trust of the infantry soldier in the addition of light weapons. From this we can understand why the purchase of the manufacturing machinery by Slavin was greeted with understanding and agreement. This purchase was in keeping with the view that the basic need was for bullets and light weaponry. Yosef Avidar notes in his memoirs that the turnabout in the aims of the Haganah only took place in 1947:

One may regard the month of July 1947 as the date which marked the major turnabout in the overall perception of the Haganah.

---

[200] See: "Mei"Haganah" LiTzeva Haganah (From the "Haganah" to the Defense Army), pp. 242-267.

This turnabout was the beginning of the transformation of the Haganah from a military settlement organization to an army[201].

The turnabout took place with the background of internal power struggles in Ben-Gurion's party and in the Haganah High Command, the high point of this being "the revolt of the generals" against Ben-Gurion in May 1948.

On June 18, 1947, when Galili was made the Chief of the Haganah and Dori the Chief of Staff, Ben-Gurion began to implement his plan, which was later known as "the parallel organization." The central idea was to establish a sort of parallel High Command which would have only a single task: the preparation of a regular army for the future. According to this conception, the Haganah was to deal with the ongoing security maintenance, while "experienced military personnel," who had been in the British army and in the Jewish Brigade, would prepare the army of the future[202].

Anita Shapira sees this as "an attempt to exchange the elite of one army for that of another, one type of avantgarde for another type of avantgarde, an action which resulted in the development of a defense system with various injustices and with pain.[203]" Without going into whether it would been possible for Ben-Gurion's reorganization to have taken place without these injustices and pain or to enter into apologetics, as Shlomo Shamir attempted in regard to Ben-Gurion's

---

201 See: BaDerekh LeTzaHaL (On the Way to the IDF), p. 266.
202 See: Ben-Gurion, Vol. 2, p. 662.
203 See: Anita Shapira, MiPiturei HaRaMa ad Piruk HaPalmah (From the Dismissal of the Chief of Staff to the Disbanding of the Palmah), HaKibbutz HaMe'uhad, Tel Aviv, 1985, p. 64.

The Commitment

actions[204], one can say that the conceptual and theoretical struggle regarding the establishment of an army which could withstand the threat of the invasion of Arab armies had decisive influence on the arms acquisition activities outside Palestine, and especially in the United States. Had this theoretical struggle been concluded two years earlier, the arms acquisition activities would have enjoyed a much broader definition of aims and goals. The fact is that, for example, the purchase of planes in the United States was more than anything the private initiative of Al Schwimmer. It is true that Reuven Dafni writes that already at the end of 1946 he had met with Schwimmer in his efforts to recruit "Trustees," but no one, including Shlomo Shamir, who was the head of the Haganah delegation who brought in Schwimmer, denies that the Haganah Command in Palestine never demanded that planes be acquired in the United States. Only after the acquisition personnel in the United States conveyed to the Haganah Command in Palestine the possibility of acquiring planes did they begin to demand these. On October 3, 1947, Ben-Gurion wrote in his diary: "I have orders to go to America to buy planes, and to recruit pilots so that at least some of them should come to the country immediately.[205]"

Such an order had not been given two years earlier, because it had been thought to be but a pipe dream and was against the underlying defense conception. The shipments of "plane replacement parts" at the end of 1948 and the beginning of 1949 was a clear indication that this

---

204 See: Shlomo Shamir, "Al Uvdot Ve'al Lik'han" (On Facts and on their Lessons), Ma'arkhot, March-April 1985 (henceforth: "On Facts and on their Lessons"). Similarly, see, a series of articles in Yedi'ot Aharonot by Aviezer Golan, entitled "The Revolt of the Generals." April 24 and 26, 1985, and May 3, 1985.
205 See: Ben-Gurion, Vol. 2, p. 660. From Ben-Gurion's Diary, October 3, 1947.

type of activity could have been carried out to parallel the acquisition of machining tools. It is true that this would have caused storage problems, but there were adequate solutions to this problem, both in the United States and in Palestine itself. They could have added planes to those of the company which operated in the country, or they could have launched new companies like the "Airline Services" or LAPSA, or opened a flying school in the United States to train pilots as that of Eleanor Rudnik. So too could the United States have served as a storage facility at the earliest stages.

(right to left) Deputy Aviation Minister Hai Yissachar, Chief of Staff Yaakov Dori, Aharon Remez and Hyman Shamir at the Ekron Airport, 1948

The continuation of the conceptual and theoretical struggle until the end of 1947 was therefore a limiting and restraining factor in the development of an acquisitions system which would meet the needs of the future Jewish army, which would function based on defined goals, tasks, and clear priorities for the establishment of such an army.

Al Schwimmer and Hyman Shamir in a tour of one of the air force bases

The Human Factor

The three commanders of the Haganah delegation in the United States - Dori, Shamir, and Kolleck - were not familiar with how things work in this country. Their posting was for them their first opportunity to become acquainted with the country. Kolleck's comment reflects how ill-prepared he had been:

> I knew much less about this country than I knew about England when I first arrived there, and I did not have the opportunity to gain an impression of the Americans as I had of the British, and

especially of their behavior during the Blitz. In short, I left for America very much unprepared[206].

Regarding the goals of the delegation, and the transfer of the role of head of the delegation from Shamir to Kolleck, Teddy Kolleck notes:

> When Shamir was called back to Palestine after a short time, in order to be given an officer's field position, **the task given to me was complex and undefined**[207].

From the testimony of Shlomo Shamir it appears that he understood the aim of arms acquisition to be a function of a limited threat by the Palestinian Arabs. Even though Shamir was the Commander of the Brigade and had acquired battle experience in service in the British army in World War II, he believed that the primary aim in preparing a Jewish army for battle was to prepare the individual soldier, while only emphasizing the use of light weapons[208].

According to Reuven Dafni, the definition of the assignments of the first delegation was totally clear: to purchase manufacturing machinery, to collect money and weapons, to purchase ships for "illegal immigration," and to recruit "Trustees."[209]

The expansion of the delegation's assignments regarding arms acquisition at the end of 1947 was not a function of a new definition of the delegation's assignment by the Haganah, but was the result

---

206 See: Yerushalayim Ahat (One Jerusalem), p. 80 (my emphasis).
207 Ibid.p. 79 (my emphasis).
208 When the Brigade was established, Shlomo Shamir was made its commander. See: On Facts and on their Lessons, and the interview with Shlomo Shamir, Tel Aviv, June 12, 1985.
209 See: Reuven Dafni, Testimony, Ben-Gurion University of the Negev, Beersheba, April 30, 1985.

of developments in the field, and that, in turn, was a function of the establishment of a system which was in keeping with the conditions in the United States. Each of the heads of the delegation in the United States was faced with the problem of personally adapting to a new and vastly different land, the possibilities contained within it, and the way to exploit its potential to the fullest. Unfortunately, the limited time in which each was stationed there made it impossible for them to adapt completely and to utilize to the fullest their personal abilities under American conditions. On the other hand, the frequent changes in personnel contributed to refreshing the system and to preventing stagnation. There is no doubt that the process of "Americanizing" the arms purchase system would have been more successful had it been carried out by people to whom the American milieu was first nature. At the same time, it is important to remember that the purpose of the Haganah delegation in the United States was to fulfill the demands of the Haganah in Palestine, and not of America. Thus it was essential that these people be familiar with the conditions in Palestine, and that they burn with an inner fire to fulfill the Zionist dream: that of establishing a Jewish state in Palestine. On the other hand, knowing the conditions in Palestine could lead to a false perception, that when the struggle began - if it would begin - it would be primarily a struggle between the Jews and the Palestinian Arabs, i.e., a very limited military skirmish.

Referring to the conditions at the time he completed his term of service in the United States at the end of January 1948, Shlomo Shamir had the following to say:

> No one knew in January what would be in May ... After the fact, we now know what happened in May. Up to the declaration of

the State, there were at least four declarations. I was a participant in the discussions. We spoke about the possibility that we might possibly obtain a tract of land in Cyprus where we could establish an army, or we could seal off Tel Aviv and Sharona, and if they would allocate Tel Aviv and Sharona to us we could establish the army in that section. Afterwards we pondered: would there be a State or would there not be a State? Would it be postponed? Maybe in another year? ... Our natural survival instinct in the Zionist sector did not act in a manner which would be appropriate when faced with a war for our independence. The Yishuv did not sense, like the zebras in Africa, that in the near future there would be a life and death war. I very much appreciate the fact that we need another and another dunam (a land measure of a quarter of an acre), and that the dunam is most decisive, but our senses should have set the alarms ringing. Only by a miracle were we saved in the War of Independence, and only belief in God can explain it. Only a miracle saved us in the War of Independence. How close were we to almost not survive? Rationally, we had no chance of survival. We survived, concentrated forces, fought, and lost 6,000 people[210].

The survival instinct is a direct function of the preparation to confront the potential danger which is regarded as a threat in the broadest sense. Shamir was among those who assumed that even if there would be a military confrontation, it would be very limited, and as a result he was so taken aback by the force of the struggle in the War of Independence. There is no doubt that his personal belief reflected the emphases of the arms acquisition requests he received at the time.

---

210 See: Shlomo Shamir, Interview, Tel Aviv, June 12, 1985.

It is possible that the criteria for the selection of the head of the Haganah delegation in the United States were based on an analysis of the components of the position, its difficulties and the skills it required; but it is clear that the first requirement to be selected for this position was loyalty to the political party. It is no secret that extremely capable individuals such as Yitzchak Sadeh, Yigal Allon, Shimon Avidan, Nahum Sarig, Yosef Tabenkin and others were not promoted above a certain point because of ideological differences with Ben-Gurion. Dori, Shamir, and Kolleck were considered to be most talented individuals, who had proven themselves before receiving the position. Were they the best candidates for this position? It is clear that in spite of their talents and party loyalty, they were lacking certain basic skills with which they would have been more successful than they actually were.

The position of the head of the Haganah delegation in the United States was the most vital one regarding the success of the arms purchase system in the United States. The selection of men who had had no prior experience in the American milieu, the frequent changes of personnel in that role, and the lack of preparation a comprehensive arms acquisition policy as a function of the threat of a broad-scale war harmed their ability to run the system in a way as to exploit the American potential to the fullest.

The Organizational Factor

The lack of a clear arms acquisition policy created a situation where different - and sometimes strange - ventures were run simultaneously, without a sense of priorities. As the number of demands increased, the organizational apparatus also grew. The need for secrecy and compartmentalization added to the difficulties of the administrators who struggled to control everything happening in the field. Teddy Kolleck explains what it was like:

> Sometimes the lack of organization was so widespread that it appeared almost essential - and indeed the matters ran smoothly for a considerable stretch of time ... In addition to the fact that we were spread out and befuddled organizationally, there was also utter confusion in the accounting records ... Of course, the most disorderly area was that of our illegal endeavors. These matters had to be paid in cash, without receiving receipts or keeping any written records ... The legal side of our ventures - which was a considerable part of what we did - also was not in order ... Hundreds of letters streamed to our office from various people who wanted to volunteer, and many of these were from all types of weird characters, so that in the end we were rather apathetic about all of them[211].

Eliezer Kaplan, who was the Minister of Finance, also complained about the lack of coordination and the differences between those involved in arms acquisition.

> Eliezer complains about our delegation regarding these matters - where one belittles and sometimes even denigrates another. Freddie is opposed to buying Yehudah's Constellation. Yehudah denigrates Ehud. There is no cooperation[212].

---

211 See: Yerushalayim Ahat (One Jerusalem), pp. 91-93 (my emphasis).
212 See: Ben-Gurion, Diary, Vol. 1, p. 137, testimony of January 12, 1948. Similarly, testimony of Shlomo in a document sent to Ben-Gurion on March 26, 1948, Appendix C above.

Beyond the organizational growth, which was accompanied by a growing number of administrative bodies and where the coordination between them was minimal, there was also a constant problem financially. The revenue sources for the arms acquisitions were two: a) the Jewish Agency; b) the Sonneborn Institute, or "Americans for Haganah" (the purchase fund). The need for a specific fund for arms acquisition stemmed from the need to carry out such purchases secretly, and to pay large amounts in cash. This required the establishment of a separate funding mechanism from those of the Jewish Agency and of the official Zionist institutions. On the other hand, the fund was not large enough to cover all the purchases, and there was need to have the official institutions help in the funding. This condition made the fund dependent on the official institutions and caused friction with them, resulting in numerous crises. Thus, for example, Ben-Gurion wrote in his diary on December 11, 1947:

> [Eliezer] Kaplan, under pressure by Montor and Silver, demands that the Haganah fund-raising be stopped ... Silver and Neuman regard "Americans for Haganah" as an arrangement by the left.
>
> "Alon" [the alias of Yehudah Arazi, the head of the arms acquisition in the United States] is in despair. They slashed two-thirds of what had been promised to him. He cannot meet his obligations - and that leaves a bad impression on the people[213].

The discovery of the cargo in the New Jersey port brought about a renewed effort by the Jewish Agency to merge all the fund-raising

---

213 Ibid.p. 41 (December 11, 1947).

efforts. The Jewish Agency wanted to issue a public statement regarding the acquisition of arms, while announcing its responsibility for the act[214]. The crisis which faced the Sonneborn Institute brought about joint discussions with the Jewish Agency regarding the future of the fund. On January 21, 1948 Ben-Gurion wrote in his diary:

> Sonneborn and Harold Jaffer were opposed to the termination of our fund [for defense and security] ... Before the trip of Chai [Yisascharov] there was a joint meeting of the two offices [our fund and that of the "Friends"] in order to merge them. The head of the "Friends" is David Wohl. The president is Ab. Feinberg. The head of the Fund is Harold Jaffer. Difficulties emerged in the merger and in selecting a new administrator ... Ruth Berman and Alice Schulman claim that the Jews do not give them rest, and demand the raising of money for the Haganah. A number of people refuse to give to the [United] Fund, but only to the Haganah. In an artificial manner this opposition is stopped[215].

In spite of the contacts regarding the merging of the funds, the Sonneborn Institute continued to finance the Haganah coffers separately throughout the war, and even for some time thereafter.

The Sonneborn Institute and the Jewish Agency were in a constant state of tension, not only in terms of the control over the financial resources. Ben- Gurion wrote in his diary on January 29, 1948: "[Abba Hillel] Silver wanted to be the head of the recruitment in America,[216]" and Teddy Kolleck notes in his book that after the vote at the UN

---

214   Ibid. p. 135 (January 12, 1948).
215   Ibid. p. 168 (January 12, 1948).
216   Ibid. p. 192 (January 29, 1948).

The Commitment

Silver would come weekly from Cleveland to New York, to attend the meetings of the Institute and to receive direct reports from Teddy Kolleck himself[217].

It is possible that Ben-Gurion saw danger from Silver's drawing close to the Haganah apparatus in the United States. Emmanuel Neuman wrote:

> Why is there the almost unconcealed enmity between them? There was those who said that Ben-Gurion felt that Silver was a powerful opponent for the position of the head of world Zionism; maybe he was not happy about the fantastic regard and the popularity in which Silver was held. He might also have felt that Silver might use his power against the standing and influence of Mapai[218].

And Michael Bar-Zohar wrote:

> Two strong individuals like Silver and Ben-Gurion could not dwell for any lengthy period of time in close proximity without a violent struggle breaking out in regard to the leadership[219].

Either way, there is no doubt that some of the organizational difficulties of the Haganah in the United States were based on the convoluted relationship with the Jewish Agency and the official organizations, which were affected in no small measure by the tension between the leaders.

The arms acquisition in the United States was affected to a large extent by the nature of the ties with the Haganah Command in Palestine.

---

217 See: Yerushalayim Ahat (One Jerusalem), pp. 82.
218 See: Emmanuel Neuman, BeZirat HaMa'avak HaTzioni (In the Arena of the Zionist Struggle), The Zionist Library of the World Zionist Organization, Jerusalem, 1977, p 299.
219 See: Bar-Zohar, Ben-Gurion, Vol. 1, p. 555.

Whereas up to 1947 arms acquisition outside Palestine was carried out through the Jewish Agency and was controlled by the Command in Palestine, from September 1947 there were direct ties between Ben-Gurion and the Jewish Agency. The personal involvement and intervention of Ben-Gurion regarding arms acquisition starting from September 1947 can be understood given the background of the British Minister for the Colonies regarding the evacuation from Palestine, and the increased probability of a military confrontation between the Yishuv and the orderly Arab armies.

In February 1948 Shaul Meirov (Avigdor) was appointed as coordinator of the arms acquisitions outside Palestine. His appointment marked two important developments[220]:

a. The shifting of the emphasis of the Haganah activities outside Palestine from "illegal immigration" to arms acquisition.

b. The subordination of the organization in charge of arms acquisition outside Palestine directly to Ben-Gurion, while preserving coordination ties with the High Command and the Chief of Staff. Shaul Avigdor wrote about this:

The days of political and military decisions drew closer. Ben-Gurion entered totally into preparing the Haganah for the expected tests. He was very angry at me because I was still deeply involved in "illegal immigration." "Don't you sense what is happening, what is to be expected?" he asked me with open and aggressive

---

[220] See: "Mei"Haganah" LiTzeva Haganah (From the "Haganah" to the Defense Army), pp. 88-89.

displeasure at one of our meetings. But I have decided to bring the "illegal immigration" to the decisive and final stage[221].

His words express the dilemma between arms acquisition and "illegal immigration" and the difficulties to act in accordance with the new order of priorities dictated to him. There is no doubt that these difficulties were expressed in the emphases and instructions given to the task of arms acquisition and to the people subject to them.

The attenuation of the authority of the Chief of Staff regarding arms acquisition abroad finds its expression in a letter of reprimand which Ben-Gurion sent to Teddy Kolleck on March 28, 1948:

I am very angry at you. All the time I have not received any information from you except for a letter to Galili of which I received a copy ... I assigned you a mission in America. Should you not have sent me at least one report? You of course are permitted to write to whoever you want to, but to send reports only to me[222].

This letter testifies to the confusion faced by Teddy Kolleck based on the organizational change in the Haganah Command regarding arms acquisition activities outside Palestine.

The last link in the arms acquisition system, which relates to arms acquisition in the United States, is the way Yehudah Arazi functioned. Arazi was a sworn individualist, who acted in the United States and in Europe directly subordinate to Ben-Gurion. For Arazi too, the working

---

221 See: Shaul Avigur, Im Dor HaHaganah (With the Haganah Generation), Ma'arkhot, Tel Aviv, 1978), Vol. 2, p. 160

222 See: Ben-Gurion, Vol. 2, p. 163. Similarly, see letter by Teddy Kolleck to Ben-Gurion of April 1, 1948 in Appendix F, and Ben-Gurion's reply of May 15, 1949, in Appendix G.

conditions in the United States were strange and unfamiliar[223]. Eli Shalit refused to work with him[224], and others, among them Shaul Avigdor, entered into frequent confrontations with him. The failure to buy the landing craft Ito stemmed primarily from the fact that Arazi entered into a large and exciting project, which was in keeping with his nature, without understanding the limitations which the United States had placed upon the entire transaction. The broad authority which he had received for independent action above the heads of the arms acquisition delegation in the United States stood in opposition to his ignorance in the American arena. This situation regarding a person who had the legal backing for action from Ben-Gurion, creating coordination problems, and even certain redundancies, in the actions of the delegation in the United States[225].

The arms acquisition activities in the United States brought about the creation of a large organizational apparatus in its internal cells. The difficulties in controlling this apparatus, and the complexity of the relations between it and the official Zionist organizations in United States, and the Haganah High Command in Palestine, hampered the utilization to the fullest of the possibilities of arms acquisition in America.

---

223 See: Shaul Avigur, Im Dor HaHaganah (With the Haganah Generation), Vol. 2, p 162.
224 See: The Trustees, p. 118.
225 See: Yerushalayim Ahat (One Jerusalem), pp. 162-167.

Yehudah Arazi on a steamroller meant to smuggle in arms and machinery

(Poland, 1938)

Summary

The arms acquisition activities in the United States in the years 1945-1949 were a manifestation of an organized mass activity which expressed identification and loyalty to the struggle carried out by the Yishuv in Palestine. While the heads of the official Zionist organizations were occupied with political activity toward establishing a Jewish state and the solution of the problem of the Displaced Persons, the arms acquisition activities were dealt with by hundreds and thousands of Jews and Jewish youths, who in spite of being American citizens, felt intuitively the massive and decisive importance in their deeds. This feeling was expressed in the words of Al Robison, who said: "Here we had the opportunity, which might come but once in one's lifetime, to feel proud that we could actually create history. This was the greatest time in our lives, which gave us a feeling of achievement as we had never felt before, and which it has been impossible to feel ever since.[226]"

The readiness of many Jews to endanger their lives and to violate United States law in their actions in acquiring arms was a new

---

[226] See: The Trustees, p. 283 (my emphases).

phenomenon, a unique one in the history of the Zionist movement in America. None of those involved could have foreseen that the Jewish struggle in Palestine would end in victory. Their actions took place in a constant haze of uncertainty, which but emphasized the deep significance which they saw in the establishment of the State of Israel. The establishment of the State meant to them the smashing of the stereotype of the diaspora Jew; an event which would serve as compensation for the generations of persecution, a promise that those who maintained the Jewish religion could also emerge victorious, and that adherence to the Jewish religion did not need to end in further suffering. The establishment of the State meant that the Jewish People are no longer weak and helpless. The motivation for this mass involvement in the arms acquisition lay, among others, in the feeling that the establishment of the State would create a new image of the Jew, an image of might and power. Basically, the ties between the State of Israel and the Jews of the diaspora lies in the creation of the new stereotype of the Jew which is an antithesis to the old one, and thereby plants in the hearts of the Jews pride and self-respect, which they lacked for the 2000 years of the diaspora.

Even though the arms acquisition activities in the United States involved many individuals who participated in them, we must remember that the initiative for these and the leadership in their regard came from the Yishuv forces in Palestine. The thorough, secret, and extended work of the Haganah activists throughout the United States in the years 1946-1947 were what created the foundation for the recruiting of the Trustees and the operation of a broad-scale arms acquisition organization. The growth of the organization brought with it a process of Americanization, which meant an adaptation to the working conditions of America, while at the same time launching new initiatives based on the conditions which were created in the field. The Americanization process of the arms acquisition activities increased the involvement and participation of the American Jews in this activity until they were the motivational force without which the system could not survive.

Regarding the arms acquisition activities in the United States, there were two basic periods:

a. The Preliminary Acquisitions in the years 1946-1947, which dealt primarily with manufacturing machinery and "illegal immigration" ships.

b. The Acquisitions during the War Period, in the years 1948-1949, which included airplanes, communications gear, ordnance supplies, motor vehicles, armored carriers, food, gasoline, arms, and the other types of auxiliary equipment.

The policy of the United States regarding the Jewish Problem in the years 1945-1949 was hesitant, and lacked any commitment to the establishment of a Jewish state in Palestine. The American policy, the limitations regarding exports and the imposing of an embargo on the export of arms to the Middle East, all of these forcibly brought about secret and compartmentalized activities, which often entailed violations of American law. In spite of this, the preliminary acquisition activities were successful. The purchase of manufacturing machinery was the basis for the military industry in the areas of the manufacture of bullets, submachine guns, mortars, shells, grenades, and demolition materials, in the War of Independence and thereafter. The ships which had been bought in the United States or by means of money collected in the United States, brought about 40,000 new immigrants to the country between 1945 and 1949. By chance, those ships themselves, which had been purchased from US army surplus in 1946 and 1947, were the main backbone of the first naval campaign of the Israeli navy.

The majority of the arms acquisitions, and the voluntary activities in this regard, took place specifically during the War of Independence. The acquisition of the planes enabled the arms deal with Czechoslovakia and created the infrastructure for establishing the Israeli Air Force. The other types of acquisitions during the war equipped and enabled the Jewish army to be mobile in the War of Independence.

The activities of the Etzel in the United States were expressed in minor and negligible arms acquisition activities when compared to those of the Haganah, and it is possible that the lack of coordination between the two organizations even harmed some of the arms acquisition activities of the Haganah. The primary contribution of the "Committee" during that time was the bringing of the Jewish Problem to the attention of the American public and the administration, while making a forceful and uncompromising demand for the establishment of a Jewish state and a Jewish army, with the maximal assistance of propaganda and communications tools.

In spite of the victory which was won in the War of Independence, and in spite of the final success of the arms acquisition activities in the United States, the American potential was not exploited to the fullest. The main reason for this was due to various shortcomings in the Haganah High Command. The arms acquisition activities then - and today - should have been a function of the analysis of the maximal enemy threat which the Yishuv could expect during a war, by all its enemies. The perception of many leaders of the Haganah, that any "war" would be along the same lines as the 1936-1939 Arab disturbances, or possibly on a somewhat larger scale, did not take into account the invasion by Arab armies into the country. Only at the end of 1947 did the arms acquisition activities begin to reflect the maximal threat. The perceptional and theoretical struggle prevented the preparation of a comprehensive arms acquisition plan which would define goals, tasks, and priorities in the arms acquisition activities. Of course, on top of this there were the objective conditions of the Yishuv in the country, such as the British mandatory rule and the uncertainty about the future.

The war years were not utilized properly to establish a network of Trustees in the United States, which could have begun to make purchases as early as 1944. As the atmosphere prevailing during the war was not exploited, the arms acquisition activities had to begin in the period after the war, while contending with the alert eyes of the bureaucracy. The latter attempted to introduce order and discipline in every area, as a consequence of the conclusion of the war. As a result, the time needed to set up the system took much longer.

The failure to exploit the war years, along with the lack of an arms acquisition plan which was appropriate to the maximal threat, brought about the establishment of a bloated and complex purchasing organization, which found it difficult to control all its activities and to utilize the human and material resources which America offered.

An examination of the purchase system in America between 1945 and 1949 shows Ben-Gurion as a man of vision on the one hand, and as a leader subject to mighty power struggles within his party and the world Zionist organization on the other. The internal struggles and the objective limitations were the primary reasons why his words at the end of the 1930s were only realized at the end of the 1940s. The Jews of the United States indeed served as a catalyst toward establishing a Jewish army and the establishment of a Jewish state in Palestine. Had it not been for them, it is highly doubtful whether we would have seen the fulfillment of the Jewish dream in terms of the great victory in the War of Independence and the establishment of the State of Israel.

Bibliography

ספרים

אביגור, שאול. עם דור ההגנה, מערכות, תל־אביב, 1978.
אבידר, יוסף. בדרך לצה"ל, מערכות, תל־אביב, 1977.
בן־גוריון, דוד. בהלחם ישראל, הוצאת מפלגת פועלי ארץ־ישראל, 1951.
בן־גוריון, דוד. יומן המלחמה, תש"ח-תש"ט, משרד הבטחון — ההוצאה לאור, תל־אביב, 1982.
בר־זהר, מיכאל. בן־גוריון, עם עובד, תל־אביב, 1975.
ברנר, אורי. אלטלנה, הקיבוץ המאוחד, תל־אביב, 1978.
גלבר, יואב. למה פירקו את הפלמ"ח, שוקן, ירושלים ותל־אביב, 1986.
דונקלמן, בן. נאמנות כפולה, שוקן, תל־אביב, 1977.
דיין, משה. אבני דרך, מהדורת ידיעות אחרונות, ירושלים, 1976.
דרווז'י, ז'אק. פרשת אקסודוס באור חדש, עם עובד, תל־אביב, 1971.
דרזנין, צבי. היימן, האיש והתקופה, זמורה, ביתן, מודן, תל־אביב, 1980.
הדרי, זאב (וניה). אניות או מדינה, הקיבוץ המאוחד, אוניברסיטת בן־גוריון בנגב, תשמ"א.
וזה, פנחס (פיניק). המשימה רכש, מערכות, תל־אביב, 1966.
וייסגל, מאיר. עד כאן, ויידנפלד וניקולסון, ירושלים, 1972.
ויצמן, עזר. לך שמים לך ארץ. ספרית מעריב, תל־אביב, 1975.

טל, אליעזר. **מבצעי חיל הים במלחמת הקוממיות**, מערכות, תל-אביב, 1964.

טרומן, הרי ס׳. **שנות מסה ותוחלת**, כרך שני, עיינות, תל-אביב, 1956.

לאפייר, דומיניק וקולינס, לארי. **ירושלים, ירושלים**, ויידנפלד וניקולסון, ספרית מעריב, ירושלים, 1972.

לקויר, זאב. **תולדות הציונות**, שוקן, ירושלים ותל-אביב, 1974.

מאיר, גולדה. **חיי**, ספרית מעריב, 1975.

נאור, מרדכי. **ההעפלה**, משרד הבטחון — ההוצאה לאור, 1968.

ניומאן, עמנואל. **בזירת המאבק הציוני: פרקי זכרונות**, הספריה הציונית על-ידי ההסתדרות הציונית העולמית, ירושלים, 1977.

ניב, דוד. **מערכות הארגון הצבאי הלאומי — הפוגה וכוננות 1940-1944**, חלק שלישי, מוסד קלוזנר, תל-אביב, 1967.

ניב, דוד. **מערכות הארגון הצבאי הלאומי במלחמה גלויה 1947-1948**, חלק שישי, מוסד קלוזנר, תל-אביב, 1980.

נקדימון, שלמה. **אלטלנה**, עידנים, ירושלים, 1978.

סלוצקי, יהודה. **ספר תולדות ההגנה**, כרך שלישי, עם עובד, תל-אביב, 1972, חלקים שני ושלישי.

סלייטר, ליאונרד. **הנאמנים: מסודות הרכש בתש"ח**, מערכות, תל-אביב, 1971.

סקלר, מרשל. **יהודי ארצות הברית**, עם עובד, תל-אביב, 1972.

עברון, יוסף. **התעשיה הבטחונית בישראל**. משרד הבטחון — ההוצאה לאור, תל-אביב, 1980.

פעיל, מאיר. מן "**ההגנה**" **לצבא ההגנה**, זמורה, ביתן, מודן, תל-אביב, 1979.

פרס, שמעון. **קלע דוד**, ויידנפלד וניקולסון, ירושלים, 1970.

קגן, בנימין. **הם המריאו בעלטה**, דבר, תל-אביב, 1960.

קולדוואל, ר"א ומאריל, א"ה. **קורות העולם**, ערך מיכאל זיו, מסדה, תל-אביב, 1968.

קולק, טדי ועמוס. **ירושלים אחת**, ספרית מעריב, תל-אביב, 1979.

קמחי, ג'ון ודוד. **דרכי סתר**, ג'רוזלם פוסט, ירושלים, 1955.

רייך, ברנרד וגוטפלד, ארנון. **ארצות-הברית והסכסוך הישראלי-ערבי**, מערכות, תל-אביב, 1977.

שחן, אביגדור. כנפי הנצחון, עם הספר, תל-אביב, 1966. (הספר נכתב על בסיס עבודה לתואר שני לאוניברסיטה העברית בירושלים.)

שיף זאב והבר איתן. לקסיקון לבטחון ישראל, זמורה, ביתן, מודן. מהדורת דבר, תל-אביב, 1976, הערכים: א. "אבק", עמ' 17 ; ב. "בלק", עמ' 80-81; ג. "חסידה", עמ' 218; ד. "עציון", עמ' 403; ה. "רכבת אווירית", עמ' 485 ; ו. "רכש", עמ' 486-487 ; ז. "שוימר, אל", עמ' 501 ; ח. "שולמן, נחמן", עמ' 502 ; ט. "תעשיה צבאית", עמ' 546-549.

שערי, דוד. גירוש קפריסין, הספריה הציונית על-ידי ההסתדרות הציונית העולמית, ירושלים, 1981.

שפירא, אניטה. מפיטורי הרמ"א עד פירוק הפלמ"ח, הקיבוץ המאוחד, תל-אביב, 1985.

שרף, זאב. שלשה ימים, 12, 13, 14 במאי 1948, עם עובד, תל-אביב, 1959.

תבין, י' אלי. החזית השניה, הוצאת רון, תל-אביב, 1973.

תולדות מלחמת הקוממיות, מערכות, תל-אביב, 1968.

מאמרים

אורן, אלחנן. "משבר הפיקוד העליון וועדת חמשת השרים בהפוגה הראשונה, יולי 1948", מערכות, 298, מרס-אפריל 1985.

ארז, יעקב. "ראיון עם אל שוימר", מעריב, 26 בדצמבר 1986.

בן-גוריון, דוד. "בדרך לצבא ולמדינת ישראל", סדרת מאמרים בדבר בין השנים 1963-1964. מאמרים: 10, 18, 22, 23, 37, 57.

בר-זהר, מיכאל. "דרושה מנהיגות", ידיעות אחרונות, 21 ביוני 1985.

גולן, אביעזר. "מרד הגנרלים", סדרת כתבות בידיעות אחרונות, 24 באפריל 1985, 26 באפריל 1985, 3 במאי 1985.

גנין, צבי. "המאבק המדיני ערב הקמת המדינה", סקירה חודשית, אפריל 1975.

מילשטיין, אורי. "ראיון עם חיים סלבין", דבר השבוע, 19 בינואר 1973.

מילשטיין, אורי. "ראיון עם חיים סלבין", **דבר השבוע**, 19 בינואר 1973.
מילשטיין, אורי. "ראיון עם אליהו סחרוב", **דבר**, 22 בספטמבר 1978.
סחרוב, אליהו. "כך הוטסו המרסרשמיטים", **הארץ**, 5 במאי 1965.
קניוק, יורם. "הבגידה הגדולה", **מעריב, סופשבוע**, 19 באפריל 1985.
שמיר, שלמה. "על עובדות ועל לקח", **מערכות**, 298, מרס-אפריל 1985.

ארכיונים

ארכיון תולדות ההגנה

אליהו סחרוב — משלוחי ציוד צבאי מאמריקה, מסמך 1202.
דוד נמרי — עדות, מסמך 4396.
ינובסקי יעקב — עדות, מסמך 4955.
ויליאם הורוביץ — עדות, מסמך 4063.
הטסת אווירונים מאירופה, מסמך 1318.
הטסת 'המבצרים המעופפים', מסמך 4685.
תיק בן-גוריון — תיק מס' 17, מברק לשרת.

ארכיון צה"ל

הרכש בארצות-הברית — 2521/50, תיק 51.
הזמנות בארצות-הברית — 254/50, תיק 64.

המכון למורשת בן-גוריון

תזכיר מה-2.7.1945 — הפגישה אצל סונבורן ב-1 ביולי 1945.

ראיונות ועדויות

סעדיה גלב — עדות, 30 באפריל 1985, אוניברסיטת בן-גוריון.
סעדיה גלב — ראיון, 22 במאי 1985, רחובות.
ראובן דפני — עדות, 30 באפריל 1985, אוניברסיטת בן-גוריון.
ראובן דפני — ראיון, 11 באפריל 1985, הרצליה.
שלמה שמיר — ראיון, 12 ביוני 1985, תל-אביב.

Appendices

Appendix A: Notification of the registration of the Hebrew Committee of National Liberation as a foreign agent

Appendix B: Memorandum of the meeting between David Ben Gurion and Rudolf G. Sonneborn, 1 July 1945

Appendix C: Letter by Shlomo Rabinowitz (Shamir) to Ben Gurion concerning the appointment of Teddy Kolleck as head of the delegation to the United States, 26 March 1948

Appendix D: Proclamation of the Etzel concerning the arrival of the Ben Hecht in Palestine

Appendix E: Hechalutz Organization of America's certification of Hyman Shechtman's flying hours

Appendix F: Teddy Kolleck's letter to Ben Gurion, 1 April 1948

Appendix G: Ben Gurion's letter to Teddy Kolleck, 15 May 1948

נספח א

נספח ב

UNITED PALESTINE APPEAL

MEMORANDUM

Date July 2, 1945

To: Mr. David Ben Gurion

From: Mr. Henry Montor

Subject: Meeting on Sunday, July 1st.

As a reminder for your records, if you should wish to have it, I am sending you a resume of the names of the people who were with you on Sunday, July 1st, 1945, at the apartment of Mr. Rudolf G. Sonneborn.

Rudolf G. Sonneborn, New York
Harold J. Goldenberg, Minneapolis
Julius Fligelman, Los Angeles
Shepard Broad, Miami
Philip Lown, Lewistown
Eli Cohen, Lynn
Ezra Shapiro, Cleveland
Albert Schiff, Columbus
Aler Lowenthal, Pittsburgh
Charles J. Rosenbloom, Pittsburgh
William Sylk, Philadelphia
Sam Zacks, Toronto
Sam Cherr, New York
Jacques Torczyner, New York
Max Livingston, New Haven
Robert Travis, Atlanta
Adolf Hamburger, Baltimore

In addition to yourself, others present were:

Eliezer Kaplan
Reuben Zaslani
Meyer Weisgal and myself.

The several individuals who undertook to act as liaison with you are Rudolf G. Sonneborn and Sam Cherr, New York, Shepard Broad, Miami, Harold Goldenberg, Minneapolis and Julius Fligelman, Los Angeles.

נספח ג

26.3.48

אל: בן-גוריון
מאת: שלמה ר.

יעקב עם הליכתו לבי"ח בקשני לסדר את הענין הבא:

מניעות ידיעות (האחרונה מפי יץ שחזר מארצות הברית)
שרות ברמן וויקטור אברונין חותרים תחת מפקדו של תדי קולק כראש
משלחת באמריקה. התירה מתבסאת בדבורים בין העוברים נגדו,
היסטריה כללית, ואי ציות להוראותיו.

על תדי עצמו אוטרת האינפורמציה, שהוא עובד קשה
וכנסה כסדר יכולתו להחזיק את הענין ביד.

לידיעתך, ויקטור אברונין לא נשלח לאמריקה כחבר
משלחת אלא מכיוון שנפל על עצמו תפקידי קניה מטעם אגף האפסנאות
(יוסף ר.) ומפני שקנזועיותו ההנדסית הוכנס לחלק פעולותיה. הוא
למעשה נסע בשם סולל בונה.

יעקב ר. מציע שאתה תתערב בדבר. ישנה גם הצעה
(ולדעתי מפוקפקת) שדוד הכהן שנמצא כיום שם יקבל על עצמו את
הנהלת המשלחת ותדי יהיה עוזרו. מסופקני אם דוד יוכל להתמנות
לכך אולם יתכן וכדאי לברר אפשרות זאת.

הצעתי היא שתשלח למשה, אישית, מברק סודי או מכתב ע"י
שליח כדלקמן:

נודע לי שאין תדי מקבל את מלוא העזרה של רות וויקטור במשלחת
ואין הם מקבלים עליהם את מרותו. אבקשך לברר את המצב ולהודיעני
ואם תמצא צורך בכך, אחזיר את רות ארצה ואודיע לויקטור סימפסיק
לטפל בכל ענין הנוגע למשלחת. כן הודיע דעתך על מנויו של
דוד הכהן כראש משלחת.

נספח ד

ההעפלה והמלחמה

ביאה של האניה "בן-הכט" ("אבריל"), על שש מאות מעפי־
לים הזורמים, שנערכשה ע״י שליחינו וידידינו מעבר לים, שמ־
קץ לעלילותיהם ולהתרברבותם של המתיימרים להיות בע־
לי־מונוסולין על ההעפלה.

ההעפלה — שבגנו הייגו יוזמיה ומארגניה הראשונים
בזמן שאחרים קללוה כ"אנרכיה" — תימשך, ארלם בניגוד למתחבקים, ל-לא נבד־
את העם באטסים הסיסמא, "מעפילים יעפילו", כי האמת היא, שההמפעלי־
לים עף-לים אך אינם עולים. הם מגורשים ע״י המשעבד בחוקיד לאיי הגהר־
ומושב להם מיבאני קבוצה-קבוצה במסגרת של מיכסת ב״ין הארורה.

ההעפלה — ויחי מארגנה אשר יהיה — היא חיזון היסטורי־
ב-מגיר, ומוכיחה את הכמיהה הבלתי־מגונצחת של המוני העם
למולדת־ה. היא גם סוללת את הדרך בשני כוחית השחרור
שייתערי בבוא היום על חופי המולדת ודרוכים לקרב ב־י־
יד ב־ריחיים בחזית הפנימית. ארלם אסור להסעית את הדע־
ה. בתנאים הקיימים אין ההעפלה לה עליה הפעמ-ית ת־א
בכוחים של מעפילים מחוסרי מגן לפריץ את השערים.

**את השערים נפרוץ ואת המולדת
נשחרר במלחמה משולבת של
שבי־ציון, לוחמיה ובוניה.
המעפילים יעפילו —
והלוחמים ילחמו!**

זורי הדרך, ובה נלך.

הארגון הצבאי הלאומי
בארץ־ישראל

נספח ה

HECHALUTZ *Organization of America*
1140 BROADWAY   MUrray Hill 5-7613   NEW YORK, N.Y.

הסתדרות
החלוץ
באמריקה

June 8, 1943

TO WHOM IT MAY CONCERN:

    This is to certify that Hyman Shechtman was a member of the flying group sponsored by our organization. We further certify that the hours of cross-country flying (see attached sheet) were logged by Hyman Shechtman on the aircraft NC38225 and NC38795 belonging to the Hechalutz Organization, and are correct and in accordance with our records.

    The entries of 9-4-41 to 9-12-41, inclusive, are those of a cross country flight made by Hyman Shechtman and Percival Tolchinsky from Windsor, New Jersey to Detroit and Cincinnati and return. The time recorded here is that flown by Hyman Shechtman.

    Respectfully yours,
    Frances Foster
    Executive Secretary

Training Farms
HECHALUTZ FARM
CREAM RIDGE, N.J.
Phone: New Egypt 4529

HECHALUTZ FARM
HIGHTSTOWN, N.J.
Phone: 545J11

החלוץ עובד
לפני המחנה

נספח ו

1 באפר ל, 1948

לבן-גוריון היקר,

מאז שקבלתי את המנוי ואת ההאר של מרכז המשלחת, שלחתי מספר דוחים לכחנהם של יואש והלל, ואני מניח שהם הוברו אליך. המכתבים האלה נגעו בבקר, מצד אחד בשאלות מעשיות בשטחים שונים, כגון: גיוס, מסודנמים א"ם, סדר והסמם של סיולהנו הצנורית כאן וכו׳, ומצד היום נשארחי ללא תשובה לרב שאלוחי. גם בכפיות בוסרות ביוחר כגון הצעות בשםת המרד, שהן מרהיקות לכת, כמו רצפת סטריו שליה כחב אפריס לאהרון ואני להלל, ונוסף כל כך הברכחי, לא אושרי אפילו קבלות הודעותינו, וכן בםעמים רבים, וזה מביא נזק לחנינינו.

מצד שני כחבחי של ראמהי לעבודה המשלחת כאן והוסר הרכוז וההתחייחוות בהוכרהעו. גם להנין זה לא נתכבלה כל הוראה מהאר. כמו כן גם נסיונוחי להסדיר את הדברים כאן במקום, בנובחוות משה וולדרה לא נשאו פרי. הנסיון האתרין לצרף את דוד לרבוז המשלחת נכשל, היום ודוד נמצא םביד בנו"יהו בסוגוכו בשניל הבסנת המאוחד. הסדיר שפ"ה ואת אי אפשר להונייהו, ולכן אין ביכולתי להכנס לצינים ולצםל בהם. אולם המצב מחייב החוסם בין השםחים השוני ובדריקת החכניוח. אף סרינה לא הייתה מרשה לעצמה להוציא חלק כזה של הפחה, שאי אפשר למלאת מחדש, של רתם חבריב י–ידים ובוריר, מכלי שיהיה תיכוך להושיך – אריא רונזאנ: – לפני שבו:ולות מספר הרבצחם 2 מליון דולר להינעי אברוני: בכשיו נתח מאבריב חכניה יפיה אסם "כויה הצעיפיו לו סכום נוסף באוחן וגדרל. נדמה לי שפר היום אברוני לא חפם את רציונה המצב, כי למ"עה הוא סוד לא שלח גלגל אחד של מכונית אחת. ובימים אלה, שיש חשם לטפור בפני בלוקדה מוחלםת של האנגלים, אי אפשר לחכנס לשכל סיד את הטביוניה םסמורות חנמצאות ברשוחו, ולא ללחת אחרי חכניות גדולות שאולי חוגשםנה רק בקבור שבועיים מספר, חדושה סניום לוסד בוסראל. גם בכחינה זו סםקי, לא טבינוב אח גדרלה. יוצאיון סכוםים כאלה של כסף צבורי בצדרה סוירים חכניים בלתי ברדר, אפילו מכלי לנזקח לויים אנשים מסדרני ראשיונה המכירים את הסקום כאן יוחר ברב לש צ בצוע םםלוה הדסלקיות האלה.

ב"יוח דוםה ישנן עם אלון ואלם שכמשלוחי.י יוחר קשה להגיב לסחוף םאשר בחנייים גלויים ובסל אברוני". חי הוא היחיד המבצע את תכניחו. אין יוצאה אניה בלי חולוחי. הדאגה היחירה אן היא חסלה הזהירוח, וגב בםעם זה חיחה צריכה להייח בסתות מרכויה, כי הםכבה היו גדולה שדמ"לא כאן בםצב הנוכחיתנצל את ההגואהוח שאנו ליכים לבצוח.

אני מסוה שאתה מבין אוהי חיעב, שאיננו שואף להבקיד חמוב יתר – לחסך, מחיה מאוש אם שלחתי אדם מחאים לקבל בידי את הנינים יסר בוום, לסרות כל הקטייים במצב, כםי שנדנמה לי הם הרבה יוחר כסורים מסה נוכן שקבלתי כאן והבדרים אוחים. הנני מוכן גם שלא לחודנ את הםקום ולהחסחר להגד הלינים דריןחדר כאן שנחם אוכל להושיל דל לדבר: זוד איננו בוכן, – לחמרא "מרכז המשלחח" בלי כהובת סבודחה כאן, שחאנה לכל םשאלוחי ובלי סוכיה םיניעלית כאן במקום.

אני בכונה נמני מלחסור לך נכחבי זה כל בנה דברנ כ"ייטים, די החוםית של םנח לי לורוש םשחולך אל חם הנדרה של החמצאח םי"לות ארגון ההנגה כאן בחרום, וחקר ביננו וכין הםרכז באוק-י"אראל.

נב"ם

נספח ז

בסוד 371/הסב
15.5.48

אל: תדי קולק
מאת: ד.ב.ג.

הנך מתבקש בזה להחזיר מיד לארצות הברית כערכך מטלחת ההגנה שם.

עליך יהיה לתאם בין השליחים הזונים, לטנוע כפילות ולפטוק ולהכריע ולתת הוראות בשעת הצורך.

על כל שליחי ההגנה בארצות הברית לקיים אתך מגע קבוע, למסור לך דוחים סדירים על עבודתם ואת הוראותיהם שהארץ יקבלו באמצעותך.

עליך יהיה לקיים קשר קבוע עם הח' לוי שקולניק והוא יטפל קנועות בשאלותיך ובשאלות שליחי ההגנה האחרים.

www.ingramcontent.com/pod-product-compliance
Lightning Source LLC
Chambersburg PA
CBHW080338170426
43194CB00014B/2605